VANCOUVER
SAN FRANCISCO
LOS ANGELES
MEXICO CITY
PANAMA
LIMA
SANTIAGO
PACIFIC OCEAN

New Zealand
and its people

New

PONY CLUB RIDERS IN WHAKAREWAREWA FOREST.

N.Z. Forest Service. Photo by J. H. Johns.

Zealand
and its people

by
Errol Brathwaite

A. R. SHEARER, GOVERNMENT PRINTER, WELLINGTON, NEW ZEALAND—1974

Photographs by New Zealand Photographic Studios.
Layout and design by B. J. Bridgeman, Government Printing Office.

FRONT COVER: MITRE PEAK, MILFORD SOUND.
BACK COVER: A NEW ZEALAND FARM SCENE.

Foreword

Earlier this year I went on an adventurous journey—not to the wastes of the Antarctic or the high peaks of the Himalayas—but amongst the valleys and mountains of my native New Zealand. I had five vigorous companions—men who had proved their strength and skill in a score of tough corners. With canoes and an inflatable boat we challenged the wild and beautiful rapids of the Hollyford River and emerged battered but intact into Lake McKerrow, nestling between high mountain ridges. We used driftwood and a tent fly to rig a spinnaker sail and roller coasted for 30 miles down the lake ahead of a fierce mountain wind, and ground to a halt on a sandy island near the lonely West Coast.

We heaved our loads onto our backs, and all day headed south along the coast into the teeth of a gale force wind. The mighty ocean rollers were sweeping up the sands with terrifying force and I have rarely felt less significant. We plunged inland again up the narrow gorges and dense rain forest of the Kaipo River, making considerable height. We turned a last corner in the valley and stopped with a surge of excitement. Ahead of us was our objective, the Kaipo Wall, a mighty unclimbed rock face filling the head of the valley.

It proved a formidable challenge. A tough struggle with steep rock, slippery ice, and heavy loads, but in the end we stood triumphant on the crest. Then hastily dug a snow cave and weathered a ferocious storm for three long days. When we finally emerged back on the road we were scruffy, dirty, and unshaven, but glowing with pleasure from the adventure, the excitement, and the beauty.

I have always disliked those who say that this or that is the most beautiful or most spectacular place they've ever seen. The world is full of beautiful places, all worthy of enjoyment. But few places have as much to offer as the countryside in New Zealand. If you are tired of the rush and smell of big cities you can spend a lifetime drifting from one glorious beach to the next. If your soul revolts at the things that man has done to his brothers, and to his environment, you can lose yourself in primeval forest or pitch your tent beside a mountain lake, and never see another face. For those who like the excitement of a challenge there are mighty mountains, foaming rivers, and rolling surf, and if your requirements are less demanding and you only want a bit of peace, a good suntan, and a comfortable home, you can get that too.

I could live anywhere if I wanted to, and there are plenty of good places to live, but I like it here in New Zealand. Its my home of course and that means a lot, but there's more to it than that. I enjoy the out of doors more than anything, and that's one thing New Zealand has a great deal of. I spend lots of time in other countries but, for me, New Zealand is a good and peaceful place to come back to.

SIR EDMUND HILLARY, K.B.E.

Contents

Prologue

In the beginning there were no people. Aeons after the older lands had felt the presence of man, New Zealand was uninhabited; just the land, spreading wide, thrusting high, with lakes like captive seas, silent in the midst of the eternal forests. Remote from the great land masses, it knew neither mammal nor marsupial. It had seen its share of saurians, all of which had long since gone, save only the streamlined little lizards and the small tuatara, last of the dinosaur race, with his sculpted, miniature tyranosaurus head. Birds ruled these islands.

Yet, because nature is a thing of delicate balance, the age old, immutable, natural systems had to be observed. There had to be preying and preyed-upon, flesh-eater and vegetarian, fruit-eater and grazing creature, forest, swamp, mountain, river, lake, and plains dwellers. And so the kiwis lurked, flightless, in the midnight depths of the forest, overlooked in the daytime by the chiming tui and the fat, fruit-gorging pigeons, the tiny, insect-eating wrens and riflemen, and the acrobatic fantail. The moa, *dinornis maximus*, bigger than an ostrich and twice as stupid, strode lordly across the tussock plains, grazing the coarse native grasses like any mammalian ruminant; and, being stupid, fell prey to the great carnivorous eagle.

And then—man arrived. At first it was the moa hunters, coming out of the Pacific mists, to slaughter the moa, and supplement a diet of his flesh from the abundance of the sea. They tended to live on the plains and the flat coastal strips, and occasionally amongst the low, rolling, limestone hills. They lived in caves and rude thatched shelters. Content, while they owned the land, to accept its bounty and ask no more than a full belly, they made no permanent mark upon it before they were engulfed by time, themselves falling prey to the more vigorous, so-called "Fleet" Maoris and the classic Maori culture.

The Maoris, coming from a Pacific homeland, probably driven by the stresses of an expanding population, brought a rather more sophisticated stone age culture with them; but climate and the nature of the new land, its very difference, modified their ways and shaped their works into a unique and unparalleled way of life. To some extent the Maoris shaped the land, carving its hilltops into terraced fortresses, planting wildernesses with fruitful gardens and spanning its more docile rivers with eel weirs. But, in the main, they had to come to terms with it, rather than changing or taming it.

And then, at last, came the European—the pakeha or stranger—bringing with him an infinitely more sophisticated technology, determined, as the Maori had probably been, to reproduce his erstwhile homeland here in New Zealand. Resisted by the Maoris, and by the land itself, he still came closer than the Maori to realising his dream—and yet not so close that his culture is not distinctly different from that of his homelands.

Not least amongst the modifying influences has been the impact made on the purely European way of life by the Maori. It shows clearly, that influence, in the language. Maori words are common in ordinary "English" speech, though usually badly mispronounced. The modern Englishman or American is puzzled, for instance, by the New Zealander's habit of farewelling people with a cheerful "hooray", which would seem to indicate gladness at their departure. In fact, it derives from "Haere ra"! which means, of course, "farewell"!

The word "whare" is still used in its original sense of house or hut, but on European lips, at least, more usually refers to a rough shanty.

Maoris adopted European personal names, albeit giving them a Maori pronunciation, so that John became Hone and Thomas became Tamate. The pakeha does the same and not a few pakeha boys have been called Tahu, meaning "beloved", while Ngaio, a species of native shrub, became and remains a popular name for girls, as did Ngaere, for its beautiful sound rather than for its meaning, which is "to quake and shiver, as a bog; or to roll".

Foreign place names often pleased the Maori ear, one particular favourite being "California". More than one locality in New Zealand acquired the name in its Maori rendering, "Karaponia".

The pakeha, in most instances, mispronounced Maori place names, and in some instances, Scots settlers Gaelicised them. Thus, Otakou, named after a Maori chief, became Otago, and the hill, Kirimoko, became the Kilmog.

As in language, so in life. The New Zealander has developed a comfortable, relaxed way of life, which his Australian cousins and American friends sometimes tend to find irksome.

Undoubtedly, Maori and pakeha have influenced each other. Neither culture has absorbed or entirely swamped the other—and neither people can claim to have wrought the greatest change in the basic nature of the other. The Maori is still, and perhaps increasingly, the Maori. The pakeha is—a New Zealander of European ancestry.

The land itself has wrought the main change. Indeed, the land has determined the form of the New Zealander's dwellings, his diet, his modes of transport, his attitudes to travel, sport, and cultural pursuits.

Today he is, yet is not, English, French, German, Yugoslav, Czechoslovakian, and tropical Polynesian, in his buildings, in his farms, in his approach to his work, and in his general outlook.

It is this similarity, this sometimes obvious and sometimes elusive difference between New Zealanders, both Maori and pakeha, and their parent peoples, that gives New Zealand its distinctive flavour.

CHAPTER 1

The Land Shaped the People

The land shaped the people. They tried to
change it, but they succeeded only partially;
and since their successes were all in the same
direction, and in the same proportion, second-
generation European New Zealanders, regardless
of national background, all seem to have been the
same kind of people, similar in their outlooks.
Up to a point, of course, this was to be expected.
Yet it was so marked a phenomenon in New
Zealand that it became manifest in the manners
and modes of communities widely separated
and living in virtual isolation from one another.

One easily seen manifestation of this
phenomenon, this change which the country
wrought on its immigrants and their immediate
offspring, is the imposition of place and cir-
cumstance upon architecture.

The Maori foresook the palm-thatched huts and
buildings of his former homeland; not all at
once, but gradually, so that even when the
European arrived, 600-odd years later, round
huts of thatch on a light framework, reminiscent
of the traditional "grass hut" of the south seas,
were still to be seen in their settlements. Yet even
these differed from their prototypes, being "dug-
in" for extra warmth.

The European, often faced with building a
dwelling even though he might never have been
taught the necessary skills, looked at the
admirably simple wooden buildings of the
Maori and, one suspects, made them his pattern,

albeit unconsciously. A ridgepole resting on three posts solidly set into the ground, with barge-boards sloping down to corner posts, and the front wall set back to form a porch—it was a plan any man could work to.

Even the European houses of the sixties and seventies, the familiar T-houses, bear traces of this early simplicity. The pitch of the roof is flattened somewhat, and the height of the sidewalls increased. A passage runs down the centre with rooms arranged at more or less regular intervals on either side, and terminates in the usual and necessary offices, with the kitchen and scullery.

Thousands still stand, resplendent with fretted bargeboards, spikey finials, and lathe-turned porch or verandah posts—practical, simple, and most liveable. Maori and pakeha both live in them. They are not European, and are by no means Maori. They are New Zealand T-houses, unique and not unattractive.

It is not as if they were deliberately designed by architects for ease of construction by colonists. Indeed, when Bohemians came from the village of Staab, near Prague, to settle in the heavy, difficult land north of Auckland, they carved their farms from the bush exactly as all other North Island settlers did; but whereas the Englishman usually preferred to plant his homestead in the middle of his acres, in splendid isolation, the Bohemians built close to one another and subdivided their land so that their farms radiated out from the village thus created. Yet the houses in this European village are, somehow, just like so many of the other pioneer homesteads of moderate size—T-houses.

The French in Akaroa built homes that were mainly of wood, just as all the other settlers did;

and although their dwellings retained a subtle French flavour, a certain—chic, a Gallic jauntiness suggested with a touch of lacey wrought iron and dainty window styles, they were, as often as not, in the simple basic style of the T-house.

The Scots of Oamaru and Dunedin built solidly and generously in stone. Their gracious mansions, very Victorian, show the tough, uncompromising streak that characterises the people of the region yet; but even they never quite succeeded in building Edinburgh-in-the-south. Instead (and in spite of the sturdy grandeur of their bigger homes) they achieved a city wherein roses grew in formal gardens, in little isles of gentility and quiet, clasped in the green fingers of the native bush which still clothes the hillsides. They created small enclaves of peace, where old homes drowse to the chiming of tuis, their paths shaded by tree ferns—but, big or small, single or double storeyed, their interiors follow the simple layout of the T-house, time and time again.

The only real architectural differences between the buildings of communities once isolated from one another are also dictated by the land, inasmuch as they lie in the materials used. The Scots, having stone available, built in stone. They also built in brick and in wood, honestly and well. The French built in wood and pise-de-terre. The English built in wood, brick, and stone.

2

The Maori brought with him the kumara, that purple-skinned sweet potato. He also brought the dog, called kuri, and now extinct, and the rat, both of which served as items of food. For the rest, he lived on certain indigenous plants,

eels, freshwater crayfish, birds, and seafoods.
His life was at first semi-nomadic, for he
wandered from place to place, always within
tribal boundaries, stopping for a season close
to the kumara plantings and moving, in season,
from there through the bird forests, past eel-
and duck-rich swamps, and down to the sea.
He stayed wherever the season was propitious
for the catching or gathering of food; and his
name for village, "kainga", can be philo-
logically traced, most likely, to a phrase meaning
"place of food".

His food was cooked in an umu, which is an
oven made by digging a hole, paving its bottom
with smooth, flat river stones, building a fire
on them and, when they are hot enough, piling
damp fuel onto them, with food wrapped in
green flax baskets and burying the whole
arrangement. Food cooked thus is steamed,
retaining its full flavour and nutriment, and it
is truly delicious. The method is still used at
large Maori gatherings such as a tangi or funeral
wake.

With the coming of the pakeha, the Maoris'
diet changed. Pork, beef, and mutton were added
to the menu. Sweet corn, they developed a taste
for, and bread made from wheaten flour. The
apple and the peach, almonds, grapes, apricots,
all found great favour with the Maori; and, in
fact, the pakeha has contributed more to the
Maori diet than has the Maori to that of the
pakeha.

The European's diet has changed very little
from that of his forebears except, perhaps, in
the portions consumed and in the fact that the
diet has become simplified in many respects.
The women have become "good plain cooks",
accustomed from earliest settlement to providing
good, nourishing, solid meals.

3

EATING OUT: ". . . wine-and-dine at a restaurant."

Increasingly, today, women are becoming more adventurous in their cooking; and there are, in New Zealand, numbers of first-rate chefs, both imported and native. The days when an invitation to dinner almost inevitably meant roast lamb, green peas, new potatoes, baked pumpkin, kumaras, and a good, honest apple pie and cream to follow, are gone. Nowadays, the hostess is more likely to serve a cunning casserole, a professional and very hot curry, or a well-prepared steak. And dining out, which used invariably to mean dinner at an hotel, is now more likely to be wine-and-dine at a restaurant, or something fairly exotic in the way of a meal.

In the field of pastry-making and the baking of cakes and biscuits, however, New Zealand women are second to none. After all, if you can produce, as a matter of course, a good loaf of bread or a cake for a special occasion in a camp oven there is simply nothing you cannot do with a coal, gas, or electric range. The pioneer women had to be able to produce bread and cakes from a camp oven, or their men went hungry. It became a prerequisite for marriage-ability to be able to cook well. (A camp oven, for the uninitiated, is a round iron pot with three or four legs and a close-fitting lid. You put it in the midst of the fire, put your kneaded loaf or your cake mixture into it, heap the hot coals all over and around it, and time it by a sort of combination of knowledge and artistic intuition.)

To this day a New Zealand family gathering, wedding, or what-have-you is fed, at some stage, with an incredibly various array of plain and fancy cakes, fudges, meringue-pavlova cakes, pastry, scones, biscuits, pikelets, and tarts.

4

HARVESTING CORN: ". . . food is very plentiful . . ."

FOOD PRODUCTION: ". . . big business."

New Zealanders, *en masse*, do not care too much for exotic foods as everyday meals. Food is primarily fuel. It must taste good, without too much seasoning, and there must be plenty of it. Cuisses de Grenouilles Frites, polenta, and risottos are fine when you are having a night out, and when you are in the mood to try something new. And if you are travelling overseas, shark's fin soup, a genuine Madras curry or escargots are tried with gusto, as part of the delight of foreign travel.

But New Zealanders, by and large, are satisfied with the foods common to the land. And that is just as well, since food is very plentiful, and its production occupies the working lives of a good many of them. There are no New Zealanders undernourished because of shortage. There are a good many who are somewhat overnourished.

5

Indeed, preventable hunger is regarded as a heinous crime. The New Zealander accepts few excuses for it, and, individually, is as generous with his foodstuffs as international relationships will allow him to be; for feeding hungry people is a favourite crusade. The production and processing of foodstuffs for export to countries which cannot produce sufficient of their own is the basis of a large proportion of New Zealand industry and much of the country's income.

New Zealand is blessed with a temperate climate. Therefore, all the foodstuffs which such a climate and a generous, rich soil can produce form the New Zealander's diet. He would not have it any other way.

3

The pioneers, having once established themselves firmly in their isolated, widely separated areas, turned their attention to the ending of their isolation. They had to. They could, metaphorically speaking, sit about and feel homesick, and allow the alien countryside to press in upon them, and continually remind them by its very strangeness of all that they had left in their birth-lands; and, as happened now and then, destroy them. Or they could take a more positive attitude, communicate with other settlements, and direct their efforts towards creating a new nation. This most of them chose to do. But the land dictated the form of their communicating—their modes of travel.

An isolated settlement like New Plymouth, or Napier, or Masterton, was never regarded by its inhabitants as an entity, but always as part of the larger colony—and eventually of the nation—of New Zealand. People who, in many cases, never lived to see settlers from other parts of the country, planned and toiled to open and maintain contact with their distant neighbours. Bridle paths and bullock trails started where the roads stopped, and riverbeds, beaches, and Maori tracks served where the bullock trails did not go. But it would probably be fair to say that the isolation really began to disappear when the main trunk railway was pushed through.

The railway builders were as tough, hardworking, and enterprising as those of any other country; but again, the land itself decided what kind of railway they would have. It is, to this day, narrow gauge—3 ft 6 in.—because it has to wind interminably around rocky bluffs, across unstable scree slides, and over soggy swampland, and because every inch of it had to be chipped, hewn, carved, and shaped by hand. It was from the beginning a tax on the ingenuity of its builders. To surmount one mighty hill, they laid a third, centre rail, and used powerful little

BUSH ROAD: "Where the rail did not run, they built roads . . ."

locomotives fitted with internal driving wheels which grasped the centre rail and hauled engine and train uphill. To overcome gradient problems on the steep face at Raurimu, they actually arranged the track in a spiral configuration, crossing over itself by means of tunnels, to corkscrew its way to the top.

Where the rail did not run they built roads, and where there were no roads, they used sea lanes and river transport, building their own small wooden vessels.

They built their own aircraft, eventually, too. A man named Richard Pearse was the first, although it was some time before anyone followed him. Pearse was a south Canterbury farmer, completely out of touch with the main-stream of aviation development and research, around the turn of the century. Yet he designed, built, and flew a very good aircraft. There are even some investigators who believe that he did it before the Wright brothers. Certainly it was within months of their historic first flight—but his aeroplane was somewhat different, and not at all like the machines which later flew in Europe and the United States. Where the Wright's mounted an engine on their most successful glider-design, and achieved lateral control by warping the entire wing, the pilot lying prone on the machine, Pearse sat upright in his aircraft, on a seat which could be shifted fore or aft at will, on a rail, to alter the centre of gravity, and thus the trim, of the craft. He had a steerable nosewheel, a variable pitch propeller, and achieved lateral control with ailerons, as is the case with modern aircraft. The Wright's virtually threw their machine down the slope of a sand dune and achieved a few yards of wobbly flight. Pearse took off under his own power, provided by an engine he had designed and built himself, and also achieved a few yards of wobbly flight. Of course, the Wright's machine landed in one piece, more or less, as it was designed to land, whereas Pearse's first flight ended in a gorse hedge—not because there was anything radically wrong with the stability of his machine, according to modern experts, but because he simply had not yet learnt how to fly. Later, he achieved a longish flight along a winding course, following a river, at an altitude which rarely exceeded 50 ft.

Pearse's neighbours were contemptuous of a man who could neglect his land while he built what they contended to be mad, impractical, useless contraptions; but a few years later men of Pearse's age were paying £100 each to learn to fly, so that they could go to England, join the Royal Flying Corps, and fly at the Western Front during the First World War.

But flying had to happen here, if anywhere. It was, and still is, the obvious link, the most practical way of surmounting the frowning ranges and rough sea straits, to join isolated communities together. So the nature of the land, that ruggedness which made flying a necessity, and the broad, billiard table flat plains of Canterbury, and the sheltered bays and harbours of the north which provided calm seaplane landing, could be said to have made and kept New Zealanders airminded.

8

JET BOAT: ". . . operates in 4 in. of water . . ."

In this and in other things, the land shaped the people. It forced them to be original in their thinking—though this was perhaps partly because they left their European homes before nineteenth-century technology had captured their imaginations. It prevented them from following the leads of older nations slavishly. It made them pioneers in social reform and in aspects of day-to-day living. It influenced them all, regardless of social or national antecedents. It bred men like Pearse, who built, in 1903, an aeroplane possessing all the essential features of a Spitfire or Mustang; Lord Rutherford, who split the atom; Hamilton, who invented and now manufactures the jet boat, a craft that will operate speedily and happily in 4 in. of water, which is about all the depth there is over long stretches of many of New Zealand's gravel-choked rivers. It produced leaders like

Sir Peter Buck, the Maoris' beloved Te Rangi Hiroa. It made men of action like Sir Edmund Hillary, conqueror of Mount Everest, and Sir Keith Park, victorious in the Battle of Britain, who took over the defence of beleaguered Malta and turned it into a wholly effective offensive. It bred surgeons like Barratt-Boyes, and plastic surgeons like Sir Archibald MacIndoe, who did not know the meaning of the word "impossible".

The land made New Zealanders what they are, so that they do what they do in their own way.

And what are they? What do they do?

As with people everywhere, they do whatever the time of day or the season of the year demands. It is how they do it that makes them distinctively New Zealanders.

CHAPTER 2

The New Zealand Morning

New Zealand mornings begin, for South
Islanders, at 12,349 ft; (for North Islanders they
begin at the summit of Mount Hikurangi, 5,606 ft
above sea level, but 12,000 ft seems rather
more spectacular.) You can stand near the head
of Lake Pukaki in that intense dark just before
the dawn, when the moon has long since set,
and the stars, huge in this clear, high-country
air, are still bright in the far western corners
of the night; and suddenly, high above you, a
flame kindles. It grows and spreads and resolves
itself, as the eastern horizon pales and light
begins to draw itself across the sky, into a
mountain peak. Mount Cook, the highest peak
in the country, has caught the morning sun.

In the valleys and the lowlands it is still dark.
Country mornings begin with the long head-
light beams of the rural delivery newspaper van,

MILKING SHED: ". . . fitting suction cups to cows' udders."

or the yellow, unreflected, almost timid light of the milking sheds, marking little solitudes of illumination in the just-awakening dark.

The farmer, fitting suction cups to cows' udders, knows without thinking about it that other farmers are performing exactly the same tasks in the chill of the morning. He knows without thinking about it that the hour is early. If he were questioned, he would probably confess to a belief that he rises earlier, and works harder and longer, than the town or city man. He is, in this, the universal farmer.

In the cities, the milk roundsman clinks and gear-grinds down the streets beneath the paling street lamps. The first commuter trains slide in between station platforms to release the earliest workers, and to take home the retiring

night shifts, or those people who begin work early in suburban factories. In the narrow mouth of Lyttelton Harbour, on Banks Peninsula, the inter-island ferry glides into calm water, leaving the long coastal swell behind; and passengers, leaving the warmth of cabins, begin to appear on deck to watch such harbour installations as the Godley Head coastal artillery emplacements. In hospitals, cheerful nurses begin their starched, bright busy-ness.

During the next 8 hours, New Zealanders will shovel coal, fell trees, test vaccines, teach children, cook meals, drive trucks, sail ships, load cargoes, fly aeroplanes, assist ewes to lamb, perform heart surgery, service jet fighters, drive jet boats, pursue speeding motorists, walk beats, pound typewriters. They are, in all these things, the universal twentieth century people.

INTER-ISLAND FERRY: "... glides into calm water ..."

WAIRAKEI STEAM BORES: "... a Dante's Inferno of a valley ..."

It is in the small things that they are different. A New Zealand Brown or Smith will walk down his front path to his front gate to collect his newspaper and his milk bottles, and will have his cup of tea and his oatmeal before he drives off in his car—to work in a Dante's Inferno of a valley amongst gargantuan pipelines which carry subterranean steam to drive generators in a building constructed with flexible corners and floor mountings to keep the turbines on an even keel during earthquakes, which are frequent in the area.

A New Zealand Rabonovich comes in from his early morning tasks in the vineyard to sit down to a precisely similar first meal.

A New Zealand Sandy MacDonald works and directs a grey-white flood of sheep as they spill down a hillside to the yards, where he will work his 2,000 head flock through his 6-stand shearing shed.

A New Zealand Knudsen labours in his milking shed, milking his Jersey herd with milking machines, which is the way cows are milked in any technologically advanced country, but milking is done in a herringbone shed which is purely New Zealand in design—and it is the only time throughout the year that his cattle spend under a roof. They are on pasture all year round, a fact which he takes as much for granted as he does the superlative cone of Mount Egmont, in a fold of whose widespread skirts his farmstead lies.

New Zealanders work. They work on high country cattle runs, droving herds of big Herefords to the sales over roads that seem to traverse the roof of the world. They drive giant road machines and bulldozers around the walls of fierce, forested gorges. They sweat in the ruddy glow of foundries. They tap typewriters in offices. They set crayfish pots. They drive tanks.

New Zealanders play—and the range of activity is wide, including: rugby football, soccer, golf, softball, cricket, billiards, water skiing, surfing, swimming, bridge, chess, skiing, skating, scuba-diving.

NEW ZEALANDERS
PLAY.

RIVER AVON, SPRINGTIME: "... fresh ... with pale new greenery."

"NEW ZEALANDERS ... tunnel

New Zealanders ride racehorses and hunters, sail, fly, glide, drive racing cars and railway engines.

New Zealanders are tinkers, tailors, soldiers, sailors, doctors, lawyers, churchmen. They go to school, to university, to teachers' training colleges.

New Zealanders tunnel, mine, drive graders, work sawmills, plant trees.

New Zealanders pursue some activities which are peculiarly their own.

Most of them are early risers, despising the sluggard. It is, maybe, another lingering pioneer quirk. Their day begins with the coming of the sun.

"Springtime is most noticeable in the country."

2

In New Zealand, as in other parts of the world, spring is the countryman's time. In the towns the gardens begin to bloom, the motor mowers to chug, and the trees are fresh in the eye with pale new greenery. People notice and admire; and the girls step out in new, flimsier finery, and the young men buy new suits. August, when the northern hemisphere summer is beginning to tire, and the days are apt to be drowsy hot, is here a month of quickening. Spring is hard on winter's heels.

New Zealand's historical springtime still lingers in the hearts and minds of the middle-aged and elderly. It was a time when, Maori-Pakeha wars over, new ventures were begun. The towns grew with just a touch of Edwardian elegance in the larger centres. The nation started to make its mark on the wider world; and, internally, the growing network of roads and railways was one aspect of that legacy from the pioneering era—the self-reliance and the conviction that a man can do anything he turns his hand to. It was a conviction and confidence that carried the nation through two world wars, when the people's patriotism was strengthened by a certain quality of life which did not depend on national prosperity.

Plenty of people who are still alive and working knew the era intimately, and some cities are full of buildings of the period, the mock-Venetian palaces which house insurance companies, and the solid, heavily elegant, confident office blocks, banks, shipping company buildings. That historical springtime made its greatest mark on the larger towns and cities.

But the year-by-year springtime is most noticeable in the country. There are lambs in the paddocks and daffodils on the hillsides. The whole country takes on that new, fresh, slightly damp look, and even the drops of last night's rain on the fence wires have that jewel-like sparkle that winter water lacks.

Yet the countryman does not see these things; or, rather, he sees them through different eyes. The shepherd rides "around the ewes" in late July and early August watching for cast sheep held down in a hollow, on their backs, by the strangling weight of their own winter wool, and perhaps by their unborn lambs. His horse, or his Gnat vehicle, goes unheeding through the green, white, and gold carpet of daffodils and snowdrops—unheeding because it takes concentration to see a lambing ewe in difficulties across a rain-veiled gully. Or he scrambles up

hills still greasy-wet where the early spring frosts have been melted by a suddenly fiercer sun.

This is the time of quick hailstorms, numbed hands, and a wet saddle. Winter is still not so far away, still capable of lashing back petulently with hard frosts and, perhaps snow, to blast the earliest fruit blossoms and kill newborn lambs. (it is axiomatic amongst New Zealand farmers, even in the warm northern districts, that lambs are always born in appalling weather).

Later in spring the lambs are docked; a sharp, efficiently performed operation done swiftly and matter-of-factly in temporary yards, often in the midst of some of the most gloriously scenic country in the world. But with a couple of thousand lambs to dock and ear-mark, a farmer does not have much time to admire the scenery.

Even so, that same farmer is no less susceptible to beauty than anyone else. It is all a matter of familiarity. He tours, during his holiday, to about the same extent as anyone else; and he, like anyone else, will stand and gaze in silent rapture at the blossom-laden pear trees in a Stoke orchard, or at the rumpled, snow-coated face of the Remarkable Range giving back the moonlight like a mirror across Lake Wakatipu.

". . . blossom-laden pear trees in a Stoke orchard . . ."

CANTERBURY: "Nobody . . . lives far from mountains."

But then the orchardist is blasé about blossoms and apprehensive about the snow which refrigerates the night air; (nobody south of Northland lives very far from mountains).

The farmer, as it happens, is a perfect example of the way in which the land has moulded and changed the people.

On the Canterbury plains the land is flat, easy, and richly alluvial. It positively begged its settlers to spread themselves on vast sheep runs. Moneyed people, the younger sons of great or rich families, retired anglo-indian civil servants and soldiers, and already rich Australian squatters, took up holdings of hundreds of square miles. These were later broken up, somewhat, to encourage closer settlement; but, even so, Canterbury farms tended to be big, running to tens of thousands of acres.

Because the fortunes founded on and supported by these holdings permitted of a more than merely comfortable standard of living, sons were encouraged to take over the farms when their fathers retired. Some of them spent more time in England and Europe than they did in New Zealand, directing managers by mail. They regarded themselves as English, often enough.

New Zealand farms range from smallholdings, intensively farmed for sheep, cereal crops, potatoes, pigs, and dairy cows, to large sheep and cattle runs of thousands of acres.

Perhaps because some of the original owners were younger sons, excluded from ownership of ancestral English acres by primogeniture, they saw to it that their own younger sons shared in their New Zealand holdings. The big farms were subdivided among offspring who certainly did not want to be divorced from such rich soil; and, with constant subdivision, fluctuating prices for farm produce, and various other economic factors, more intensive farming became the rule as Canterbury farms became smaller and smaller—a mass, in some areas, of smallholdings, carrying sheep, cereal crops, potatoes, pigs, and dairy cows. The Canterbury smallholder, often a lineal descendant of those sheep moguls of the nineteenth century, became the nearest New Zealand ever had to a peasant farmer, in the very finest sense of the term; a man who knew his acres intimately and loved them—who was a little close and clannish, often barely acknowledging the world beyond a 20-mile radius, and concerned with keeping his small farm economically viable, come drought or flood. Today, the pendulum is swinging back. His grandchildren know rather more of the world than their grazier grandsires did—and farm more efficiently still.

The true peasant, that Scottish crofter who came from his native highland mists to the Canterbury high country, a land of equally bitter climatic extremes, saw the great sheep stations in those areas broken up. Canny and thrifty, he showed himself to be a good manager for his absentee employer; and as legislation, drought, snow storm, scab outbreaks, and half a hundred other recurring vicissitudes convinced the owner that high-country farming was not such a paying or permanently good proposition as farming on the rich plains, sons and grandsons of former highlander shepherd-managers began to acquire the land they worked

on. Today, their descendants own and operate the high country runs—the last really big sheep runs in the country.

The Canterbury farmers' story has been repeated in reverse in south Otago, where Scottish settlers acquired smallholdings and raised mutton, milk, pork, and poultry to feed the armies of men engaged in timber felling and milling in the great native pine and beech forests in the area. They carved their farms out of the forest, and they built their homesteads close together, to form—not villages, precisely, but fairly close communities. They built school houses and churches near their straggling settlements, and for a while they did reasonably well. But the millable timber was soon worked out to the point where further cutting would leave the hills unprotected from the eroding rains, and the trade dwindled. The little farms, deprived of local markets, were no longer viable, and neighbour sold out to neighbour, who in turn sold out to neighbour. The little farms became big farms and the big farms bigger yet. The little houses and schools and churches still stand, empty and forlorn, grazed about by sheep and fat cattle.

Somehow, though, the smallholder's approach has prevailed—or all that was best in it. The south Otago farmer thinks big, but in his work and his stock and pasture management he is a careful husbandman. The area is virtually free from stock diseases, and the hillsides, protected by sufficient timber to hold them together in the area's high rainfall, are fat pastures.

In Taranaki, in the North Island, in the land wars fought with the Maoris in the 1860s, farmers became soldiers, founding in the process one of New Zealand's most famous infantry regiments—whereas, in the Waikato, soldiers occupying buffer territory between hostile

SHEEP SALEYARDS.

The motorbike has often replaced the stock horse.

Maoris and nervous Pakeha settlers, became farmers, and have since often been innovators and leaders in the dairying industry.

And the Maoris themselves have become farmers. This might seem strange, for "farmer" implies ownership and exclusive use of a respectable acreage of land, whereas the Maori approach to land has always been that of common ownership. Their land belongs to the people, rather than to individual persons.

In this they have not really changed. Instead, the Maori has taken a leaf from the book of the Pakeha businessman and formed incorporations to manage land which, often enough, has lain idle for 100 years or more. The Mangatu Incorporation near Gisborne, half way up the east coast of the North Island, farms 96,000 acres in contiguous sheep stations. The Ngati-Whakaue Incorporation at Rotorua is big business in any man's language, with assets probably in the region of $5,500,000. Nevertheless more and more individual Maoris are becoming successful dairy farmers, independent of incorporations. This is not exactly a new burst of enterprise, but it is a growing thing.

But, Maori or Pakeha, there is a sameness about New Zealand farmers. The farmer in this country is traditionally the man who can do anything. He quite often repairs his own machinery. In remoter districts where the horse is still used he shoes his own horses. He kills his own meat and dresses it for the table. He builds his own buildings and erects his own fences—miles upon miles of post, wire, and batten fences, running over broken country in lines so straight they might have been professionally surveyed. He doctors his animals, knowledgeably administering vaccinations and inoculations with a hypodermic syringe, and worm drenches with special "guns". He masters the somewhat complicated mathematics of pasture control, drench, animal husbandry, and financial budgeting. He knows the virtues of his clovers and grasses, knowing that originally, most of them have been sown, the coarse native grasses being less palatable and nutritious. He works tremendously hard, and often enough enjoys about the same standard of living as a small-to-middling businessman— a comfortable home, radio, television, a good car, a well-spread table, and maybe an occasional holiday trip abroad.

AUTUMN, POHANGINA VALLEY, MANAWATU DISTRICT: Typical grazing land.

SUMMER OAT HARVEST, QUEENSTOWN.

DEERSTALKER OVERLOOKING LAKE WAIKAREMOANA, UREWERA NATIONAL PARK.

The city dweller who gazes out from his red morning bus at the daffodil-carpeted woodland of Christchurch's Hagley Park would probably envy him and envy the forestry worker, too, measuring his seedlings in the heart of the Tokoroa Forest. The forestry worker, a corner of his mind still idly planning his next summer yachting holiday in the Hauraki Gulf, might envy the trawlerman cruising down the Kaikoura coast. The trawlermen, their little ships rising and falling on the long coastal swell, where migrating whales sometimes surface and blow on their way south for the summer, probably glance towards the towering seaward Kaikoura range, still snow crowned, and envy the deerstalker or the pig shooter, pushing his way up a high valley to the heart of the mountains, far from cold salt water, fish, and the stench of diesel oil.

There is a warmth in the sun which encourages dreaming, in spite of winter's occasional rear-guard actions. It coaxes the vegetables and flowers to spread themselves over the soil of suburban gardens, and tempts the Sunday drivers out from the cities to see the fresh green of the country, and the yellow kowhai blossoms

FOREST STREAM, EARLY SUMMER.

like little golden scimitars, and the new and
friendlier sparkle of the sea.

But spring is still the countryman's season. It
does not really impress itself with any fervour
upon the dweller in grey asphalt, characterless
concrete and brick cities.

Nor does it belong to the wild native forests.
New Zealand trees are predominantly evergreen,
and the bush is not noticeably fresher in the
spring.

Summer is the time of the forest's greatest
glory.

27

3

In summer the floor of the forest is warm,
with a—not dryness, for the deep leaf mould
is never quite that—but moist rather than
saturated; and the fantails snatch the small,
emerging insects in mid air, and the pigeons
fatten visibly on hinau berries.

The hills' coating of forest is an infinity of olive
shadings splashed with red rata blossom, and
starred with white clematis.

Except in the very south-western corner of the
South Island, the forest is inhabited by men.
They are the last of the pioneers, these men,
being tough, self-reliant, and strong, not
needing the signposts and constant reassurance
of familiar streets and landmarks. They trudge
incredible distances and even drive a variety
of motor vehicles over country which has never
and probably will never be traversed by anything remotely resembling a road. Some of
them are deer cullers, sharpshooters, working
over allotted blocks of country, thinning out
the deer population as an erosion control
measure. Some are guides, taking visiting
American and Japanese businessmen hunting.
Some trap opossum. Some fell timber. Some
prospect for gold and even more precious
metals in secret valleys in the high ranges.

Some are surveyors. Some are farmers. All of
them walk the twisty trails and stride over the
razor-back ridges as other people walk the
streets of their towns. The same easy familiarity
is apparent.

The forest is sparsely dotted by their shacks,
pioneer dwellings indeed, built of slab and bark
and corrugated iron lugged painfully from the
nearest roadhead. They are built to keep out
the sluicing high-forest rains and to keep in the
warmth of the night fire; big enough to
hold three or four bunks, a crude table, and
perhaps a meat safe. Incredibly, you will sometimes find a cast iron range in a bush shack.

Yet the bushman does not own this shack,
built though it is with his sweat and his
peculiar skills. Not in the sense that the
suburbanite owns his home, anyway. Maybe
the bushman did build it, or helped to; but it
is there for the use of all who roam the forested
hills. It does not worry him that strangers
are using his hut in his absence. He knows what
they will be like. They will be strong, methodical,
clean men, like himself. There is a sort of simple
code that they all follow in these matters. Use
the shack if you will, but leave it as you found
it down to the last stick of firewood; and close
it securely against the destructive opossum when
you leave.

TRAMPERS, SOUTHERN ALPS: ". . . walking twisty trails and . . . razorback ridges . . ."

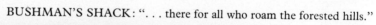
BUSHMAN'S SHACK: ". . . there for all who roam the forested hills."

Summer is a drowsy time in small New Zealand towns. The grass grows tall and brown in creviced verge of pavements, streets are almost empty, cicada-loud in the late-morning heat, perhaps a little dusty, and there is a somnolence, an enjoyable peace which the traffic of the cities does not allow. There is, above all, the certain feeling that you can, whenever you feel like it, go and take a plunge in the river, or do something positive to cool yourself—because there is no city stuffiness here.

Summer is the children's time, also. Every season is the children's time, but summer and

winter especially, because they are the extremes, the times of richest difference, colour, and uncompromising heat and cold; but summer is their favourite.

The beach is perhaps the most popular playground, for nearly all of them, in these slim islands, live close enough to the coast to spend at least part of their summer holiday on the papa reefs and the sand, and in the long, easy surf which is tamed by the continental shelf.

The children's summer holidays begin mere days before Christmas and continue late into summer, in the first days of February.

New Zealand children on holiday own the land. They sail fat little yachts with a beam almost equal to their length. They flog placid streams like Christchurch's Avon or Waipukurau's Tuki Tuki, or the Waipa, willow-choked and narrow as it wanders through the lush Waikato, flicking out their wet or dry flies and catching brown trout which they wrap and stuff into their clothes and carry unconcernedly throughout a whole, long hot day. Or they clamber amongst the piles of a handy wharf, past the rust-streaked flanks of ocean-going ships, with a lead sinker and a couple of hooks on 50 ft of string to fish for herrings. New Zealand children ride ponies to the shearing muster in the spectacular King Country hinterland. They get underfoot at agricultural and pastoral shows, and sit on the seats of demonstration tractors, making engine noises and twisting the steering wheel to and fro. Small, brown Maori children and small European children, tanned almost as brown by the summer sun, ride the lifts to the top floors of city buildings, and dodge irritated janitors by descending via 12 or 14 flights of stairs, fill school and public swimming pools with shrill chatter and much splashing and shrieking, risk life and limb on swings and parallel bars in public park playgrounds.

Their summer morning begins early, because even 16 hours of high summer daylight is barely enough for all that they have to do.

CHILDREN, LAKE TAUPO "... play with floating pumice ..."

New Zealand children are about the same as children anywhere else—except that the harbour on which they sail their yachts is likely to be the crater of some ancient volcano which exploded with titanic force in the morning of the world; and the lakes on which they row, and in which they swim and fish, are likely to be drowned valleys of ice-age glaciers. They make the sparkling waters laugh beneath this latter-day sun, or they scramble over hoary old lava, or play with the floating pumice pebbles of more recent eruptions unthinkingly, mindful only of their world's potential as a plaything.

The summer mornings begin early for others beside the children. Coastal shipping takes small account of the clock, regulating its comings and goings by tide and perhaps by weather. If the right tide for quitting a river mouth port occurs early in the morning, the seamen work up a sweat long before the landsman has had first thoughts about leaving his bed.

Before ever the first sleeper of the first stretch of New Zealand railway was laid—years before the first rough bullock tracks began to link the roads together—the little ships of New Zealand plied its rugged coastline. Ever since New

THE LITTLE SHIPS: ". . . comings and goings by tide and perhaps by weather."

Zealanders have been building little ships superbly, and New Zealand seamen have been sailing them.

Little ships they have had to be. Iron sands of Taranaki, and the scrap iron of generations of machinery, have so far been insufficient to nourish heavy industry. There are sizeable foundries, and there are engineering shops which make a certain amount of light machinery and components for heavy machinery, and there are assembly plants which put together cars, machinery, and aircraft. The industrial worker is usually fairly versatile, having a good working

THE KIWI ARTISAN: ". . . a fund of skills in metal-working . . .'

HYDRO ELECTRIC DAM, MARAETAI, WAIKATO RIV

knowledge of more procedures than the one on which he is currently engaged. Lathe workers, for instance, have a fund of skills in metal-working from marking out to bending, drilling, and general fitting. Specialisation is probably increasing as the size and output of factories grow, but the engineering workshop man is still apt to be something of a Jack-of-all-trades.

The kiwi artisan has supreme confidence in his own abilities. More often than not, it is well placed. He could do many things which he has not yet tackled on a large scale. There is, for example, a budding aircraft industry. Aircraft of New Zealand design have been built, and aircraft of overseas design have been modified, improved, and marketed to the world as a New Zealand design. Given capital and a ready supply of certain components it is possible that New Zealanders will, before long, equip their own air force and civil airlines with first-line military and civil aircraft. There is probably

room for a good cargo liner design for New Zealand conditions too. There are designers, engineers, and artisans who could build them. They have already built big locomotives, hydro-electric dams, ships, bridges, and a great network of railways and an even greater network of roads.

Probably, though, our most skilled artisans are our woodworkers. Wood, is our medium. New Zealand mullet boats built of wood are fine examples of the shipbuilders' craft—functional, workaday ships which would double happily as pleasure yachts, graceful of line and docile. Coastal vessels of less graceful but equally functional design are built to slip over the sandbars on Westland rivermouths, and to cope with occasional huge seas off the low-lying eastern coasts. They carry timber and tallow, cars and cases, machinery and steel roundstock, or whatever else is more conveniently sent from port to port than by road, rail or air.

Fishing boats include sturdy little craft which poke graceful bows into some appallingly narrow gut on a wave-swept reef and are hauled up by winches onto rocky shores at day's end.

The history of New Zealand boat building is a long one, considered as a part of the history of the country. The Maoris, having settled in New Zealand, soon lost the art of building the great, double-hulled ocean-going canoes which brought them from Hawaiki; but they constructed vast war canoes, waka-taua, for coastal and river navigation, employing in the process all of their considerable skill in woodworking. And the very first European mission activity, at Paihia, in the Bay of Islands, was to build a little schooner to carry the gospels up and down the coasts. She was commissioned by the Rev. Henry Williams, who had enjoyed an earlier career as a naval officer, and knew a trim craft when he saw one.

There was really never any need for bigger ships. Fish are abundant close in, and cargo carrying has always been purely a matter of redistributing the bounty of the land, rather than of imports and exports. Naturally, New Zealand does import and export—lives by its trade, in fact; but this sort of cargo carrying is handled by New Zealand and overseas shipping companies whose ships are built in the great shipyards of the world. The coastal vessels and fishing boats and pleasure yachts and launches and jet boats are most purely New Zealand's own. We understand small ships.

Take, for example, the fishing sailor, standing in his tiny wheelhouse as the sun heaves itself over the tilting horizon, warmed by it early as he envelopes a chipped enamel mug of power-ful tea in his blue hands. He is a good, weather-wise, and resourceful seaman.

The chances are that his great-grandfather chased whales in the Marlborough Sounds or in Cloudy Bay, and fathered sons who took to pursuing smaller game when the whales were almost slaughtered out of existence. This may have given rise to an attitude which makes the New Zealand fisherman different because he is conservation conscious. He seldom thinks of it in exactly those terms, but the idea is there. Take what you need, and what the market can reasonably consume, and no more. Therefore, the operator who attacks the Foveaux Strait oyster beds with a scientifically designed, highly efficient dredge, on a ship with all facilities for shelling and packing, is apt to be frowned upon. There is a proper, fair way of getting oysters, oyster fishermen will say. We have always satisfied the market until now, and we expect to continue to do so. A little shortage once in a while keeps the value up anyway. And that's that.

It is an attitude with a lot to commend it where conservation is concerned.

Even that other professional sailor, the navy man, is a small-boat man, whose fisheries protection ship is little more than a large launch. He performs his tasks with good humour, in the main, although he reacts to discomfort and petty annoyance in much the same way as any other man reacts to it. He is, essentially, a workman, doing a job which, for all its occasional distasteful moments, is what he wants to do. He wears his uniform, when he wears it at all, unselfconsciously and without either arrogance or overbearing humourless pride. He works hard, perhaps a little harder than he is often given credit for, because his equipment is usually old, and he must make it perform minor miracles.

FISHING BOATS, WELLINGTON: "We understand small ships."

LANDING FISH, WELLINGTON: "Take what you need . . . and no more."

There are, incidentally, sailors in New Zealand who operate professionally yet seldom go near the sea. They are the launch skippers on the great lakes—the men who carry sightseers on Lakes Rotorua, Taupo, Wanaka, Wakatipu, Te Anau, and a dozen others. They sail deep waters, especially on the southern lakes which are often well over 1,000 ft deep; and they know the moods of wind and weather. Lakestorms can be every bit as dangerous as storms at sea. They are shrewd, competent men, well used to handling people *en masse*. Their fathers often sailed the same waters, before the days of diesel or petrol engines, when tourist launches were driven by steam, the same as any other self-respecting Victorian machinery, and tourists had to be landed fairly frequently and cajoled into collecting firewood for the boat's boiler furnace.

Summer mornings see the New Zealand policeman driving through suburban streets, on his way back to the central police station after a night's car patrol. He is maybe a touch more self-conscious in his blue uniform and peaked cap; for whereas the navy, army, or air force man finds in his life and his job points of considerable similarity to the lives and jobs of certain civilian counterparts, the policeman does not. Other men sail launches remarkably like fisheries protection launches. Nobody else cruises around the city streets throughout the night, engaged in the arduous business of keeping the peace.

Summer is the time for bringing cattle from the high-country stations like Molesworth to the sale yards. They are a special breed of men who herd the beasts over the high, scree-scarred ridges, men who are accustomed to living through hard winters at the back of beyond, when the roads are covered feet thick with snowdrifts, or the rivers are high, swift, and impassable at the summer fords. They still use horses and, occasionally, landrovers and ancient army trucks which have the stamina and the four-wheel drive which will get them over the nightmare tracks bulldozed along the high, steep slopes.

"EARNSLAW," LAKE WAKATIPU: "Sailors who . . . seldom go near the sea."

POLICE CAR: ". . . driving through suburban streets . . ."

Driving, incidentally, is another thing that the New Zealand professional transport man does exceptionally well. The kiwi bus or truck driver is a man with an unshakeable confidence in his own skill. He learns to drive early, and he is, perhaps, the last of the do-it-yourselfers to be found in large numbers amongst city dwellers. He has not had to cope with the volume of traffic, nor to flog along at the speeds encountered on the freeways and turnpikes of larger countries. He has thus had time, from his youth, to observe the road, to examine its makeup, and to know how well its component parts stand up to wheeled traffic, and how close he can safely

go to its edge, and what sort of grip deep shingle has on a turning wheel. He knows the motor vehicle intimately too, his first car, often enough, having been side-valved, with magneto ignition and hand-set throttles, the jalopy of his teen years; and although the modern truck engine may have eight surprisingly small-bore cylinders arranged in a V-formation with overhead valves, and a mass of brightly-coloured and shiny ancilliaries packed around it, it holds no mysteries for him, even now. If he is middle aged, he probably drove a battered army truck in Libya and the back roads of Italy. If he is younger, he has been well taught. He will tackle

COUNTRY ROAD ENCOUNTER:
". . . time to observe the road . . ."

its ailments in any degree of emergency, sure
in the knowledge that all it needs is petrol and
a spark to get it going.

He is a driver who will unhesitatingly manoeuvre
a bus load of tourists on a narrow hill road,
getting it about-faced in three swift to-and-fro
sweeps. He is a man who drives his enormous
articulated vehicle, piled high with wool bales,
around back-country mountain roads, high
above tumultuous rivers, full of happy confidence because he knows its centre of gravity
to a hair's breadth, and he knows exactly how
far it must lean before it will tip. He knows it

43

all so well that it is never at the forefront of his mind, but simply trips a little warning bell somewhere in his system if it begins to lean too far on a tricky bend.

In this regard he is exactly like the bulldozer driver pushing a road through the southern mountains, backing to the exact safety limit on a shoulder of bulldozed earth, or crawling up an acutely angled slope. The bulldozer man tends his own monstrous machine, advises his engineer-boss on the replacement of track links or injectors, and regards it almost as his own invention.

They come from the small country towns, these drivers, or from city suburbs. They have a country background, farming or farm contracting, or an army background—which indicates only that this is how they came to discover in themselves a liking for driving heavy vehicles. Obviously most of them do like it because they are almost without exception educated sufficiently to hold a much softer job, not uncommonly having enjoyed 3, 4, or even more years of secondary schooling. They are almost invariably cheerful, courteous, and the most skilled drivers you will find anywhere.

They are, today, exactly the same stamp of men as those who first travelled the rude, late nineteenth century roads and ended the provincial centres' isolation forever.

SUMMER PICNIC: ". . . a time of family outings . . ."

Summer in the small country towns is a time of family outings—collect the children straight from school and head for the river for tea.

Summer is the roadman's time when solitary, bearded, friendly men are found wandering along the Westland roads, pushing shovel-laden bicycles, or pausing to put finishing touches to a road recently cleared of last night's slip by bulldozers, and needing the last of its scars covered with a few shovels of gravel from the road's shoulder.

Summer is shearing time on the sheep farms. It is a time of choking sheepyard dust, and oven-like shearing sheds where Maori and Pakeha shearers work all day, bent double over squirming, stiff-necked Romney or Merino ewes.

Summer is a tired time in the cities, a time when street-washing machines trundle out in the early Auckland morning to lay the dust and fill the morning air with a warm, wet, earthy scent.

". . . heads for the nearest beach . . ."

AUCKLAND STREET: ". . . a warm, wet, earthy scent."

Summer is a time of agricultural and pastoral shows, of show rings paraded by fat, slab-sided beef cattle, fawn and black Jersey bulls, plump ponies, beautiful hunting horses and polo ponies, and still, endearingly, by great Clydesdale draughthorses with braided manes and tails.

Summer is warm to hot to humid.

These islands are blessed with a marvellous climate, though, being an island climate, the weather is capricious. But it sends New Zealanders out of doors on every possible

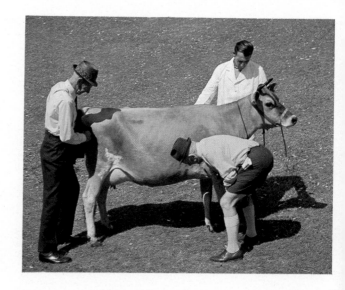

CAMPING: "The camper throws up a tent . . . and achieves an amazing degree of comf

occasion. The New Zealander expects to get into shorts or bathing trunks at the beginning of his summer holiday, and to remain in them until it is time for him to go back to work.

He does not take his holiday at home, if he can help it, but heads for the nearest beach, river, or lake.

He is usually looking for solitude. He is a crowd man just for so long as he can take his crowds in small doses, although he does not always realise or admit to this. His ideal holiday is one in which he "gets away from it all," from the kids next door, the dog that barks down the street, the smell of motor traffic, and the pressures of urban living. He camps, or he caravans, or he baches, and he does so competently. The camper throws up a tent, contrives cooking arrangements, and achieves an amazing degree of comfort in a short time. He organises his and his family's day just to the extent that water is fetched, spuds are peeled, chores are done, and everyone is able to spend the maximum time at play. The caravaner or the bach-tenant does the same. The New Zealander is supremely confident of his innate ability to make himself comfortable in any outdoor environment.

POHUTUKAWAS, COROMANDEL COAST: ". . . a great selection of semi-solitudes . . ."

Thirty-odd years ago, if he drove his family 30 or 40 miles from home to a bach beside the Pacific Ocean, he obtained a large measure of peace; because, of the few other families who possessed cars capable of negotiating the bad roads to his Shangri-la, and who could afford a bach at the beach, most were either close friends, or people who enjoyed the kind of holiday he enjoyed. It was thus near enough to isolation, and there was no question of over-crowding. At the most popular beach resorts there would be from 12 to 50 families who owned baches, and these subdivided into groups who kept to themselves.

Isolation, taken when you feel like it, is a priceless treasure, and those New Zealanders of 30-some years ago who could afford it have been apt to regard it as being everlastingly available. In recent years, however, it has become apparent that, while there are still miles of beach and lakeside and riverbank for everybody, the resorts *are* becoming more crowded.

The New Zealander, having grown up with the reassuring knowledge that there is a great selection of semi-solitudes at which he could recharge his spiritual batteries, is suddenly

KAITERITERI, NELSON PROVINCE: "Good roads . . . have brought more and more people."

ON THE COAST: ". . . near enough to isolation."

finding that good roads, better cars, and increasing affluence have brought more and more and still more people to the traditional retreats for the long weekends and summer holidays. So crowded are they becoming, that their one-time habitues are searching farther and farther afield, heading for the southern lakes or the Bay of Islands, or Mount Cook, or Lake Taupo—places which not so long ago were the kind of spots the average New Zealander visited once or twice in a lifetime, on a honeymoon or special occasion. But they are now finding, at these places, bus loads of tourists from countries which have no solitudes

left at all. So the real solitude seekers, those kiwis who have come at last to the realisation that the empty spaces they used to enjoy are filling up, are finding other places, such as the south Otago beaches, sweeps of bush-backed, golden sand, on a coast alive with fish; or the Tararua Range ski field, no chrome-plated resort, but a developing field where there is still room for the fun skier and the non-competitive amateur; or a high-country valley where there is a glider club camp, and the thermals rise fast over the vast gravel beds of rivers, and the only other people nearby are of like mind, in love with the breadth and freedom and singing silences of the clean sky. The other New Zealanders still pack the beaches, rivers, and lakesides; and these have not, for all their gregariousness, lost their taste for aloneness. They have merely had their perception of true solitary bliss blunted a little. They have not quite the same need, perhaps—yet they still insist upon building their homes in the centre of their very own quarter-acre plots of land, fenced or hedged and gardened little isles of privacy. The apartment, the high-rise block of flats, is persisting, but is slow in catching on, except perhaps in hilly Wellington or, to a lesser extent, in sprawling Auckland.

Because he has grown up in a land in which ample room is taken for granted, the New Zealander seldom if ever loses this love of solitude. It is a distinct facet of his character to the extent that he has developed the ability to be friendly and apparently outgoing without actually opening up. He seldom lets strangers know what he is really thinking or feeling. Americans in particular, those friendly and socially inclined people, sometimes express amazement over the fact that they can go to a private election-night party in New Zealand, and, at the end of the evening, still have no clear idea of how each guest voted.

. miles of beach, lakeside, and
rbank for everybody."

55

There is, by the way, another holiday activity which attracts thousands of New Zealanders of all ages. It is hop-picking and fruit harvesting. Fruit pickers and hop pickers are usually city people, lured to the hop fields and orchards by sunshine, fresh air, the warm, sweet smell of ripe apples or peaches, bright companionship, and reasonable pay. Sometimes accommodation is thrown in.

The work is not too backbreaking, not too hard on sedentary workers' slack muscles, yet tiring enough to bring healthy sleep and a good appetite. Not that they are early to bed every night. There is usually sufficient carnival atmosphere in the district to keep them entertained and wakeful, evening after evening.

These people return to their city jobs refreshed. Other seasonal workers come to the towns for off-season work as barmen, truck drivers, or anything else they can turn their hands to. These are the second category of seasonal workers, the "professional" workers, such as freezing workers and shearers.

FRUIT PICKING: "... usually city people, lured ... by sunshine, fresh air and the warm, sweet smell of ripe apples or peaches ..."

The freezing worker is well paid during the season. At a certain time of year, when the fat lambs are being sent to the works to be frozen and exported, he takes his place in the chain, slaughtering, skinning, and dressing the carcases. He works hard, and looks as if he does so, being usually a well-muscled man, powerful and fit. Maoris fill this role quite often. They are usually nuggety in build, muscular and quite tireless.

Maoris probably make up the majority of shearing gangs, too. To watch a 16 stone Maori

MUSTERING.

bent double over a squirming, unco-operative Merino ewe, removing her heavy fleece with long, seemingly effortless sweeps of his shearing handpiece is an awesome thing. He starts work early, getting into the swing of the thing before the heat of the summer's day turns the woolshed into an oven; and once he has fairly begun, neither heat nor the long, backbreaking hours seem to slow him nor to make his hand less steady. He stops around 10 o'clock in the morning to drink tea from a large mug, and to engulf doorstep-thick meat sandwiches; and then he sets to again. At midday he will tear hungrily into a substantial cooked meal. He breaks for more tea at 3 o'clock, and then sets on with seemingly renewed vigour until around 5 o'clock. A gigantic evening meal sets him up for a midnight trek of miles, to the back of the farm to catch eels in some fern-fringed creek.

His womenfolk work with him, picking up fleeces from the floor as soon as his cutter makes its final sweep down the animal's spine. They bundle each fleece carefully but rapidly, and throw it expertly, to spread it out on a slatted table for classing; and another helper folds it in a special way, with equal expertise, and thrusts it into a bin, from which it is taken by yet another worker and placed in the appropriate bale, to be pressed impossibly tight in a rachet-and-lever-operated press. Even the children help, if they are not at school, by standing inside the press and treading the fleeces down into the bale, with much leaping and laughter.

In the between seasons, the shearers, like the freezing workers, seek employment in the towns. They do not always like the towns, and they are well enough paid during the season—but

IN THE SHEARING SHED: "They . . . throw each fleece expertly to spread it for classing."

SHEARER: ". . . removing the heavy fleece with long sweeps . . ."

6 months or so is a long time to be idle. A man needs to work, if he is a man indeed. The New Zealander is uneasy without it.

4

The New Zealand autumn sees the children back in school, reluctantly indoors for five precious hours of their shortening day.

Schools in New Zealand may be classified as private (which, oddly enough, corresponds with "public school" in England), and public, or State schools. State schools comprise both single-sex and co-educational schools (most private schools are single-sex schools), district high schools which may have primary departments, city high schools, which, if they have

CANOEING: One of adventure skills taught at "Outward Bound", Marlborough Sounds.

primary departments, refer to them as "preparatory school", primary schools, and intermediate schools. There are also small, two-room country schools in remoter districts, and there is a nation-wide correspondence school for pupils who, by reason of their remoteness from other schools, or their inability to attend other schools, have to be taught at home.

School uniform is the norm in most schools. The fact is, State schools are merely provided by the State and staffed by a regional education board. They are governed by school committees of parents and teachers. Certain basic equipment is provided. Amenities such as bicycle sheds, swimming pools, and so on, are provided by parents, the fund raising usually being in the hands of parent-teacher committees, through which parents are also kept in close touch—as

close as they wish to be—with their children's progress and with trends and innovations in education. With parents having so much say in the running of the schools, it is perhaps inevitable that children should attend classes clad in clothes which are sturdy, reasonably cheap by comparison with mufti, and neat.

Probably it is the school which, next to the home, does the most towards shaping a people's culture. For school and home to be as closely inter-related as they are in New Zealand is therefore good, a strengthening influence.

The private schools are complementary to, not in opposition to, the State schools; and, in fact, they have to conform to the teaching standards laid down by the State educational authorities.

INTERMEDIATE SCHOOL: "School uniform is the norm . . ."

"Small, two-room country schools in remoter districts . . ."

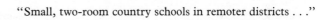

LECTURE THEATRE.

Autumn is when the days blow hot and cold, and the suburban gardeners' enthusiasm has waned, and the last cricket matches are winding up, and the first rugby players are beginning to jog around the early morning streets to get themselves fit for winter play; and the universities have begun their first term.

There are six universities in New Zealand. Not so many years ago there was only one, the University of New Zealand, which had colleges at Auckland, Wellington, Christchurch, and Dunedin; and there were two agricultural colleges, at Massey, near Palmerston North, and at Lincoln, not far from Christchurch. Today, the four colleges have autonomy. Auckland, Wellington (Victoria), Christchurch (Canterbury), and Dunedin (Otago) are separate universities to which have been added the University of Waikato at Hamilton, and Massey, which still retains an agricultural and veterinary training and research function, but to which has been added an arts faculty. (Lincoln College, however, is still agricultural, and remains a college of Canterbury University.)

Six universities, the New Zealand citizen-at-large is apt to say, are far too many for a

"A place to pursue one's chosen academic interests."

country with a population of less than 3 million. Indeed, there exists something of a gulf between student and public, which is a fairly universal state of affairs, at least in Western society. It may, however, be rather wider in New Zealand than in older countries. It is that pioneer thing again. To the New Zealand worker, university entrance is a privilege which must eventually be paid for by service to the community. So thinks the average student. The difference lies in the concepts of "service". To the man-in-the-street, one goes to university to learn to *be* something—doctor, lawyer, engineer, or accountant—or maybe a teacher or a clergyman. The idea of learning for learning's sake awakens few sparks of sympathy, and neither does the idea of the university as a place for research and development. The place for research and development is the Department of Scientific and Industrial Research, or the laboratory belonging to the chemical factory, or perhaps the agricultural colleges. But the university is properly a sort of extension of secondary school, where young New Zealanders who have done well at school, and who have a vocation or aptitude for one of the professions, go to learn their business.

To the student, university is a place where one learns to learn, and to pursue one's chosen academic interests. It is a place of liberal traditions, where freedom of thought, speech, and behaviour are sacrosanct. Understandably, it is not so much a place as a state of mind to young people fresh from the imposed discipline of schoolroom and home.

Fortunately for the general public—and, one feels, for the student—the disciplines and habits of thought prevailing in the home and in society at large are not so easily thrown off. The young radical is self-consciously radical, and being radical is, for the vast majority of students, a spare-time occupation rather than a soul-born experience.

The New Zealand student can be a long-haired young man in a rather grubby poncho, tatty jeans, and sandals, a slightly shaggy young man in shapeless slacks and an enormous jersey, a rather modish girl in a maxi-skirt, or a serious, short-haired, uniformed young serviceman, attending lectures as a parade, studying

engineering or for an arts degree on a service bursary. Students are clannish people, as university students are everywhere. They are altruistic—wear altruism like a badge at the drop of a hat. They usually worship at the shrine of originality—in everything from written expression through painting, to modes of dress and attitudes towards politics, religion, marriage, and almost everything else. To the outsider they are polite. To the middle-aged they are solicitous. With the aged they are uneasy.

But, mercifully, they are good natured. There are no bombers and shooters and hot fanatics among them. There may be some incipient cases of bloody revolution amongst the lunatic fringe, that shifting, shiftless few who always seem to be hanging about on the extreme edge of university life; but they are few indeed, and even these mostly grow up, sooner or later.

For the rest, self-conscious radicalism and originality-at-all-costs are fashions to be enjoyed. They are not deep rooted in most cases.

In the main, serious students, who go on to achieve degrees, do have some career in view. From New Zealand universities have come outstanding scientists, engineers, clerics, surgeons, economists, nuclear physicists, physicians, and chemists.

It is as it must be. Even the very young cannot entirely escape from the national character. New Zealanders are a dignified people, a disciplined people, and even the very young are uneasy when they step out of character for too long.

AUTUMN RAIN: ". . . sudden rainstorms which . . . spread water across the paved street . . ."

In autumn, the mountain people make haste to do essential maintenance of ski lifts and resort accommodation. The orchardists are busy picking and grading and packing their fruit for overseas and local markets. Farm housewives are busy putting down fruit and vegetables in freezers and bottles. Town housewives drive out into the bountiful countryside to buy ripe produce for the same purpose, and city housewives buy it by the case from markets where the glut of ripeness has brought the prices down.

Autumn in the city brings some relief from the hot dustiness of late summer. It also brings sudden rainstorms which swish the fallen leaves down gutters to build mini-dams of them, to spread water lake-like across a paved street which cannot absorb it but must hold it like a basin. The trees continue to spread their discarded finery in a litter over the footpaths, litter which is cleared away by mechanised sweepers and giant, truck-mounted vacuum cleaners, or small motor trucks carrying one man with a broom and hand shovel.

The rains creep up from the south, carried on cold fronts which were born on the antarctic ice. The last yellow harvests are gathered in—grains from the Canterbury plains and apples from Central Otago, Canterbury, Nelson, and Hawke's Bay. The ports and railway marshalling yards are busy as summer's bounty is brought in for shipment to the markets of the world.

AUTUMN SUNSHINE, WANAKA, OTAGO: "... the last yellow harvests are gathered in ..."

"... summer's bounty is brought in for shipment ..."

PICKING GRAPES, HENDERSON, AUCKLAND: "The grapes . . . for vintages little known overseas . . ."

The grapes are being crushed for vintages which are often little known overseas, yet deserve to be, for they are made with all the hard-won, centuries-old skills brought from Yugoslavia, Lebanon, Italy, France, and Germany and passed on to sons whose appearance sometimes suggests their ethnic backgrounds, but whose accents are pure kiwi.

On the rolling hills of the tamer land between mountains and sea, the autumn ploughing proceeds. It is nearly all done by tractor now, although in some of the steeper areas it might be possible to see a team of two horses and a single-furrow hillside plough. New Zealand ploughmen seldom walk behind the plough. They still win international awards but today their conversation is apt to be laced with expressions like "power take-off", "differential lock", and "weight-shift", just as any other ploughman's is. If the New Zealand ploughman differs in any way at all, it is in the crops he ploughs for; and even these are fairly universal, except, perhaps, for kamokamo, the peculiar groundvine plant whose fruit is a carelessly engaging mixture of apparent pumpkins and simulated marrows; or Chewings Fescue, or browntop, grasses which are harvested for their seed because they make remarkably smooth lawns and bowling greens.

AUTUMN PLOUGHING.

"On the rolling hills of the tamer land . . ."

SOLDIERS OF YESTERDAY AND TODAY: Anzac Day parade and soldiers in train

Autumn brings with it a sacred time, too. April is autumn's last month of comparatively mild weather—and it was on 25 April 1915, 30 long years before seaborne assaults became commonplace at Guadalcanal, Tarawa, and in Normandy, that New Zealanders, the penny of their patriotism clutched in their hot hands, stormed ashore at Gallipoli with Australians and British, to die in their thousands on the gully-riven slopes of that bleak peninsula. The 25th day of April has been kept ever since as a day of remembrance for all New Zealanders who have fallen in foreign wars. Veterans all gather at Cenotaph or local war memorial, a silent crowd of solitudes, standing quite still, with eyes filled with rememberings as they watch the dawn scrabble up the eastern sky;

old men, sparse-headed, who remember the African veldt at the turn of the century; and men who seem equally old, remembering the Gallipoli scrub or Flanders mud; and middle-aged men who recall Libyan sand and Korean snow and the jungles of fierce Pacific and Asian actions. Maybe this is one of the reasons for the so-called generation gap. Fathers and sons of four or five-generations have shared a mighty and searing experience, albeit some 20 years apart. But there has been no general mobilisation of the nation's manpower for war for thirty years, and the feeling and bond of deep mutual understanding and shared experience that today's fathers have with their fathers is not shared with the sons.

SOUTHERN WINTER: ". . . snowstorms not infrequently cover the ground . . ."

SKIERS, CORONET PEAK, OTAGO.

5

Winters are, generally speaking, mild. In the high country and in the deep south, snowstorms not infrequently cover the ground, disrupt traffic and bring down power lines, never for more than a week at a time, and seldom more than once in a winter. Perhaps for a day or so, traffic in hilly Dunedin slackens because it is dangerous to try to drive on the frozen, steep surfaces. But in the cities at least, a snowfall creates a sort of holiday atmosphere. People speak kindly to each other, and exchange cheerful, rosy-cheeked, mock-rueful comments.

But frost, now; that is different. The city milkman does not enjoy frosts. His truck is probably hard to start, and does not care to idle properly, and its windscreen keeps freezing. Early morning vehicular traffic, forgetting that he is on the road, sometimes comes too close for comfort—and an icy asphalt road is no surface on which to execute frenzied leaps to safety. The milkman is almost bad-temperedly loud on the stillness, the somehow heightened silence, of morning air which rings with cold.

Train commuters from the Hutt Valley and from the west coast townships and cities arrive in Wellington while it is still dark and the stars are huge and bright in the clean sky. They come by trains, which slide in between the station platforms punctually and surprisingly quietly, and depart again with as little fuss, trains alternating on up and down lines with a frequency that would be frightening, considering the numbers crammed into those carriages, if it were not for an efficiency which is so unobtrusive as to seem unremarkable. For the railways are, generally speaking, efficient. They probably have their off moments, when baggage goes astray, or goods are damaged in transit, but surprisingly seldom, considering the volume of traffic they carry.

The New Zealand railwayman is a self-contained creature. He usually joins the service straight from school, often as the son of a railwayman. He is educated—or perhaps re-educated—by the service; and he has to be, for the railwayman lives in a closed circle, a curiously complete little world in which exists at least three trade unions. It owns its own houses, builds much of its own equipment, trains its own tradesmen, operates its own communications systems, builds its own bridges, culverts, and viaducts—even operates its own accounting systems, not quite like any other. (During the Second World War it even raised its own unit which went to the Middle East to set up and run a military railway system.)

Winter mornings see businessmen hunch their shoulders, tuck briefcases and morning papers under their arms, and bury their hands in their pockets as they stride out across the puddled tarmac at Christchurch or Mangere International Airports to the day's first inter-city flights, while youngish men in dark uniforms and white caps walk around the aircraft, carrying out for safety's sake almost the same pre-flight check that Richard Pearse must have done, examining control surfaces, tyres, flaps, a visual check, extra to the already painstaking inspections by trained flight mechanics.

The New Zealand pilot probably does not differ too much from any other pilot, unless it is, once again, in the matter of pioneer-bred resourcefulness, and a refusal to accept the improbable as being the same thing as the impossible. He has been like this since the earliest beginnings of aviation in his country, having seldom had, ready-to-hand, the facilities that in other countries are taken for granted as being absolutely necessary to get an aeroplane into the air, and to keep it there.

Railway and airline, even more than road and motor vehicle, ended the isolation of many settlements in this ruggedly mountainous country.

AERIAL TOPDRESSING: "New Zealand pilots pioneered agricultural aviation . . ."

New Zealand pilots pioneered agricultural aviation—and this in a country which, to say the least, is mostly hilly to mountainous. They did it, at first, with a variety of war surplus aircraft, notably the ubiquitous De Havilland Tiger Moth, but also with a range of other single-engined and twin-engined aeroplanes of various vintages and ages. They even built some rather strange but wholly remarkable aircraft from the component parts of a variety of other, less suitable machines.

These farm aviation pilots have frequently turned mechanic, rigger, and airframe fitter on some back-country paddock. One pilot, landing downhill, downwind, because that was the only possible approach to the only site anywhere near suitable as a landing strip,

overshot slightly, hit a tree stump, and fractured the lower wing main spar. He contrived a repair with fence battens and wire, and flew back to base for more conventional attention.

Airline men have ample servicing facilities, naturally, where the most up-to-date maintenance and checking equipment is available. Their safety record is phenomenal, especially so in a country where most routes take them over hundreds of miles of rugged alpine country, in a capricious island climate.

It is the crop duster who enjoys the most spectacular flying, of course. The air force fighter pilot storms around the skies at the most spectacular speeds. The passenger transport pilots fly aircraft of the most spectacular sizes (the little Vickers Viscount turbo-prop

Loading fertiliser into an aircraft of New Zealand design.

aircraft flown for so long by New Zealand National Airways Corporation is roughly the size of the World War II Flying Fortress, which was, in its day, considered a big aircraft. It is quite small by comparison with today's Boeing 737 which has taken over the leading role on New Zealand's main internal airline).

All the pilots, whether smartly uniformed airline men, blue-grey overalled, crash-helmeted air force flyers, or slacks-and-sweater agricultural pilots, share that look, that air, which comes from a confidence in their own competence. It is seldom, if ever, manifest in a swagger, or any shade of arrogance. It is hard to be arrogant when you fly daily in the shadow of stupendous mountain peaks, or over an unbroken expanse of ocean.

On a winter morning in a thousand bakeries, steaming, fragrant loaves are loaded into vans for early morning delivery to a thousand surburban grocery shops. A million reluctant school children are washing and brushing and being called for breakfast. Tired train crews are making their way home after a night's interminable journeying through whistle-stops, (called "flagstations"), and goods shunting yards.

On a roadside in the Urewera forest, a Ministry of Works roadman pokes sticks into a thermette to boil a cup of tea, having been out since before dawn, clearing a minor slip on the road; and a climber, high on a mountainside, emerges from his hut, breathing on his hands, stamping cold feet, and watching gratefully the red winter sun as it slides up out of the clouded horizon.

"THE BACKBONE OF THE ISLAND . . ." The Southern Alps, a chain of peaks and ridges, some 53 of which, at heights exceeding 9,000 ft, are snow-crowned all year round.

On the Lewis Pass, northernmost pass over the main divide between east and west coasts of the South Island, an Automobile Association patrolman drives his Landrover over the top of the pass to help improvident motorists who have attempted to drive over the backbone of the island in mid-winter without chains. New Zealanders, on the whole, are not a snow-conscious people.

CARPENTERS, HOUSEBUILDING: ". . . spend their working lives engineering with wood."

Frost, they know, from Auckland clear down to the Bluff. Throughout the country, builders stand stamping and blowing and chafing cold fingers beside braziers, reluctant to handle rough wood, jarring hammer, or unforgiving plane or saw; or they could be using riveting guns, welding torches, frigid steel girders and wire-rope crane slings, because even though high-rise building has become commonplace in New Zealand only over the last 10 or 12 years, the techniques and skills required for its erection are not wanting.

Yet the majority of builders still spend their working lives engineering with wood. They do it cleverly, with remarkable skill, erecting amazingly large and complex structures with hammer-and-nail carpentry; because they, of all New Zealanders, have what is probably the longest tradition of all the country's trades.

The builder begins to learn his trade at school, at woodwork classes, where he practises cutting and fitting mortice and tenon joints, dovetails and mitres, and learns how to care for his tools. Before he begins his apprenticeship, he has learnt how to stone his chisels to a razor edge, and how to drive a nail true with half a dozen confident strokes. He knows something of the characteristics of woods, and how to put a uniform bevel on an edge.

Like all good tradesmen, he is fascinating to watch. He sets timbers straight or true by eye, using his square or his level to confirm

HIGH-RISE BUILDING:
"... the techniques and skills ... are not wanting."

rather than to determine. He saws through
four-by-twos with unhurried strokes, and
chisels mortices cleanly, quickly, and accurately.
The erection of a house becomes a well-learned
routine— the careful carpentry that goes into
setting up boxing for the foundations, the
equally careful eyeing and levelling of plates
and floor joists, the rapid prefabricating of wall
framing, set in an incredibly short time into
position. The builder understands, and quickly
accomplishes, the bracing of a roof to with-
stand the thrust of the winds, and he weather-
boards the walls with neatly mitred corners.
He makes it all look easy, and perhaps for him
it is. He also builds with bricks and with
concrete blocks, and a variety of cladding
materials, but perhaps he loves and understands
wood best of all.

"... carving of quite astonishing beauty."

Wood, you see, was always the universal material in New Zealand. There was always so much of it, and so little, often enough, of good building stone. The Maoris, besides building their houses and immense war canoes of it, made weapons and tools with it, embellishing all they did with carving of quite astonishing complexity and beauty. Wood housed them, defended them, cultivated their crops, caught their fish, speared edible birds in the forests, trapped eels in the rivers. Their stone age was really their wood age.

And, of course, the Europeans, in their turn, tore the great kauri trees from the northern forests to serve as masts and spars for their ships—and so huge and straight and branchless are those leviathan trunks that a demand for them grew amongst the seafaring nations of the world. So wood was the country's first commerce.

The settlers used readily available wood for their houses; and, as their towns sprang up, they began to replace V-huts and other forms of

KAURI TREES:
". . . huge, straight, and branchless trunks . . ."

rude shelter with the kind of buildings, wooden buildings, that they had known at home. But, the settlers, being Europeans, were ill-at-ease with wooden public and official buildings.

Stone was used for these where it was to hand—Christchurch's volcanic rock from the Port Hills, and the remarkable Oamaru stone, and limestone from Weka Pass in North Canterbury—but where it was not easily obtainable, they learned to use wood cut to resemble stone.

Every man, in the less settled areas, built his own house. Today, almost every farmer has built a shed or cottage at some time or other, and often the city or town dweller may build a garage for his car or a house for his few hens.

Wood paved Wellington's main streets until quite recently. Wood built our small coastal ships. Wood is still one of the most valuable crops in the land.

"Crop" is the correct expression. Vast exotic forests have been planted, mostly radiata pine, which grows phenomenally here, and these forests are being harvested by men who work all their lives at farming trees.

LAKE TEKAPO, MACKENZIE COUNTRY, SOUTH ISLAND: ". . . razor-backed
ridges and lonely, sub-alpine valleys."

Winter is not a time of shortage, generally
speaking. There is still plenty of meat. The
market gardeners and orchardists and farmers
have filled the nation's larders; (in favoured
Northland, you will find fruit being offered
for sale in roadside stalls in mid-winter). Cows
are still in milk, still out in open pasture.
Shooters, both amateur and professional, still
bring in venison and wild pork from razor-
backed ridges and lonely sub-alpine valleys.
Shooters who are strictly amateur go out in the
month of May and, before dawn breaks, take
up positions in maimais, hides screened with
manuka scrub and reeds, to await the early
flight of ducks. They are governed by strict
rules in the interests of conservation—only one
gun in a maimai in a condition of instant
readiness, no automatic loading guns or other
devices which give them more than two shots
between reloadings.

Sheep and cattle are still slaughtered in
abattoirs for supply to city and town butchery
businesses. Poultry is still freely available.
Fish—especially oysters—is still very much in
season. New Zealanders, then, are not a chilled,
winter-wrapped people.

CHAPTER 3

The New Zealand Noon

Historically speaking, New Zealand is probably in its florid noontide now, if only because in this world, at this time, with communications what they are, even a small nation at the bottom end of the Pacific Ocean has to grow up quickly. Certainly, New Zealand has acquired a self-confidence, looking the world in the eye and conceding nothing to the thousand years of history its parent nations can remember. There is a comfortable affluence, a conviction that we have got all we really want of the things the rest of the world has—and if we have not got certain things, we do not really want them.

Yet New Zealand still has one foot in its pioneer past, whatever may be said to the contrary—and the other foot is stepping out towards an unseeable future. The old days are changing, and the rugged, practical New Zealanders are apt to be uneasy about it.

The country's population is still small enough for a distinct "club" atmosphere to be strong here. Within his chosen work, the New Zealander often knows his counterpart at the other end of the country. If he is a soldier, he knows everyone in his arm of the service, practically everyone in the army who is of the same rank as he (if he has any), and many of his opposite numbers in the other two services. If he is a stock agent, a garage proprietor, or a post office official, he seems to be on first-name terms with most other people of his trade or profession in the country. Admittedly, this is more in the nature of an impression one gains, than a fact; but to be a New Zealander does seem very like being a member of a widespread club.

One of the things which heightens this impression is the fact that New Zealanders are wanderers. They know their own country well. Ask a New Zealander in Wellington or Palmerston North if he knows a town called Kaitaia, and he will most likely not only know it, but be able to advise you on the best pub to have a beer at in that northernmost town. Ask a Kaitaia man about the road between Coalgate and Dunsandel in mid Canterbury, and the chances are that he will have a detailed description of it, complete with a special anecdote concerning the stone church at Hororata and the rocks in the river near Coalgate. Almost everyone knows almost every place. Nobody is wholly a stranger to anyone, if he cares to let down the barriers.

a Kaitaia, Northland, man about the
church at Gisborne in Poverty Bay and
will have a detailed description of it; or
describe for you all the features of the
road between Seddon and Kaikoura, at
top end of the South Island.

The New Zealander travels abroad far more than he used to. The businessman knows his way about the world capitals, and he corresponds regularly with businessmen in Hong Kong, Paris, London, Tokyo, Sydney, New York, and Belgrade. He is aware of his own capabilities, and of his own assets, and manages to acquit himself as well as businessmen from anywhere else.

In the matter of assets, he is beginning to see in his country its real tourist potential, and is beginning at last to understand that it is better to "do our own thing" and do it.. superbly well, than to try and do someone else's thing, and do it clumsily. The impulse to create a smaller scale New York Hilton on the Milford Track is giving way to the realisation that people do not, as a rule, come thousands of miles to find a replica of home. In any case, the vast majority of New Zealanders react strongly to attempts to clutter their favourite spots with chrome and fairy lights.

By the same token, resort hotels and metropolitan hotels have acquired a new sophistication. New Zealand chefs are making the most of national foodstuffs. New Zealand cheese factories are producing connoisseur-standard cheeses, and New Zealand wineries are pro-

ducing some fine wines. Most significant, New Zealanders have come well and truly around to the view that these things are important. We have, by and large, a new definition of the word "necessity". We have finished with our pioneer morning, when we revelled in our vigour and slew our dragons and founded our fortunes, and enjoyed the warmth of a climbing sun. It still lingers, that bright morning, to the extent that we have not lost entirely those old habits of thought and speech. There are still New Zealanders who never speak of England, or the United Kingdom, but always of home, though they have never been there. Most marked, perhaps, is the New Zealand habit of clinging to the customs, manners, and even accents of ancestral homelands. The Aucklander and the Westlander speak with an almost Australian drawl. The Southlander has the remains of a Scottish burr in his speech. Throughout the land, faint traces can be discerned of a hundred regional English accents. And in what other country would you find special legislation enacted to ensure that Hahm Dahn eggs are consumed only by Chinese, whose systems are apparently better equipped to resist any ill effects from them than those of Europeans— even though the Chinese consuming them may well be third generation New Zealanders?

CITY WORKERS, LUNCHTIME: "... a brief pause to eat and relax for an hour

On the subject of food, noon in New Zealand is, as elsewhere, a time for a brief pause, to eat and relax for an hour, to gather strength for the second, more difficult half of the day.

Office workers tend to take their lunch in a paper package, the homely sandwich in the briefcase.

For the "executive" (which is about as meaningless a term here as in any other Western society), there is now the expense account or business luncheon, with wine; or perhaps a smorgasbord or a fillet mignon or a special tossed salad, dainty viands which the pioneer would have scorned as midday fare. But then, the menu and the class are both new and have no equivalent in a pioneer society.

THE OUTDOOR WORKER: ". . . even closer to the pioneer way

The true pioneer way, of course, was a substantial midday meal, designed to give a man sufficient steam to carve another quarter acre out of the virgin forest. It is still served on farms. The farmer, his family, and hands still sit down at a vast kitchen table to soups and stews in the cold months, or generous portions of cold cuts, carved off the joint by a man rather than shaved off economically by a woman or a restaurant chef, in the warm weather.

Even closer to the pioneer way is the cold - sausage, spring onions, bread and cheese and billy tea enjoyed by the rabbiter or the fencing contractor beneath the sheltering river bank or in a glade on the edge of a stand of native timber at the back of some farm. The billy, once a prerequisite for successful family picnics but now largely supplanted by the thermos flask or the thermette, is used only by rabbiters, contractors, or bushmen, now. They alone still understand it, and perform the little rituals, placing a green stick across it to prevent the tea from acquiring a smoky taste, and throwing little handfuls of tea into the water and allowing it to boil for a few moments longer.

TROUT FISHERMAN, OTAGO: ". . . pursue their real vocations only on Saturday or Sun

The New Zealand office worker is probably similar in most respects to his overseas counterpart; yet not quite the same as, say, an English or American office worker. His attitudes to his employer, his work, and his whole life-style are coloured by a strongly-felt egalitarianism. There is an independence about him, an impatience with systems that seem to contain too much detail or fuss. He approaches his work with the same self-confidence which the bushman brings to his tasks, the same conviction that, whatever it is, he can handle it. He gets impatient with his daily routine, as anyone will, but he has the comfortable knowledge that he need only tackle 5 days at a stretch, and that the weekend is the time for real living. His work supports him in the style to which he has become accustomed. The weekend is his life.

This is obviously a generalisation. There are probably plenty of office workers who find their work fascinating, and are reluctant to interrupt it. One has met such people. But it would be fair to say that the large majority of New Zealand office workers are not office workers at all, in their own minds, but gardeners who, but for some twist of fate, would be farmers; or they are yachtsmen, or carpenters, or writers, for whom chance has decreed that they shall pursue their real vocations only on Saturday and Sunday.

It is not that they dislike their work. Most would probably be acutely unhappy, or at least distinctly uneasy, if they had to leave it forever. They understand it and have found their level in it. But there is, tucked away in the back of an office worker's mind, a promise of eventual retirement, perhaps on Waiheke Island in the Hauraki Gulf, or maybe at Queenstown, or in a seaside town somewhere, or even in a country cottage in the Lansdowne Valley, near Christchurch. They do not think of retirement as a folding of the hands, but as the time when they will have earned their pension, or maybe even a modest fortune in the shape of an endowment insurance policy, sufficient to enable them to leave the office and get on with their real work, whatever it may be.

GOLFING: A popular recreation for the New Zealand worker.

Their egalitarianism prompts them to be innovators, whether they are self-employed or employees. In this they are exactly like the bulldozer driver who unhesitatingly advises his engineer-chief on maintenance schedules and parts for the machine he drives. The kiwi clerk will look his accountant employer or manager in the eye and explain shortcuts and revised systems that he thinks should be implemented.

The New Zealand industrial worker, on the other hand, is a great believer in shifts and overtime, as all industrial workers are. He would chafe at the disciplines of office or shop work. He is tied to his work for certain hours of the day, even as office and shop workers are, but he tends to feel that there is more of an element of choice in the hours. He works long hours, because the overtime pay is good—not because he has to. If he works on the early shift this week, he can go with his wife on a shopping expedition to town during the afternoon, or go fishing, or work on his car, or in his garden. Next week he may be on 4 till midnight. The following week may see him home all day, working all night. It gives him the feeling of having something of an edge on the clock-bound white-collar worker. Yet he is not so different in his attitudes and aspirations. His work is still merely the means of supporting his family and, eventually, retiring.

THE NEW ZEALAND INDUSTRIAL WORKER: ". . . works long hours . . ."

BOATBUILDING.

Actually, it is by no means unknown for the New Zealander's longing for his "real work" to cause him to give up his job, and pursue his dream. Bank managers have been known to become farmers, in their middle forties. Clerks have become market gardeners. Advertising agents have taken up raising stud sheep and cattle. Boilermakers have begun making toys. Travelling salesmen have set up as boat builders. It must be admitted that, because this is a welfare state, they stand very little chance of starving if they fail. To be just, however, they do not do it with this in mind, and if there were no welfare state, they would, in all probability do it, cheerfully remarking, "I may as well give it a go. You only live once."

The New Zealander's egalitarianism, that facet of his character that enables him to look anyone in the eye and greet him as an equal, is sometimes carried a little far, to become a sort of inverted snobbery. But this is rare, and is usually the result of an individual assuming an equality that he does not really feel. And that is not exclusively a New Zealand trait. The real egalitarianism is observable in the fact that the New Zealander, on the embankment at Dunedin's Carisbrook during a rugby match, at the races, or at the golf club, or at a ball, dresses in such a way and speaks in such a way and chooses his friends in such a way that the visitor would be unable to gain any idea of his work or profession. It would be impossible to tell from his appearance, his accents or his demeanour whether he was a professional man, a white collar worker or a factory worker.

This is not to say that he is dully uniform. He can, by his manner and his speech, be classified anywhere in the spectrum of human types, from "rough diamond" to "gentleman". New Zealanders comprise all kinds of people. It is just that they share a certain basic outlook, certain national traits, of which one is a refusal to be typed by the work they do, or even to choose their friends exclusively from within whatever social stratum their work might, elsewhere, be deemed to have placed them.

Again, this is a generalisation, but a fairly sound one. It is probably attributable to the essential similarity of most New Zealanders' backgrounds.

AT THE RACES:
"... a visitor would be unable
to gain any idea of
his work or profession ..."

Perhaps it is the small town or country background of so many of us that makes us believe
that we were really meant to live in the country,
and were not really cut out for the city at all.
And truly, every other city dweller you meet in
New Zealand "does not really belong here—
came from Waipukurau" or Taumarunui,

or Waimate. Perhaps that is why they seek out
little solitudes in which to enjoy their lunches.
In Auckland it is apt to be Meyer Park, or some
other mid-city green patch, all lawns, flowers,
trees and screening shrubs. In fortunate Christchurch it is the banks of the Avon, which slides
quietly through the very centre of the city, that

MAIN STREET, PAHIATUA: "Perhaps it is the small town background of so many of us that makes us believe we were meant to live in the country, and were not really cut out for the city at all . . ."

attracts the outdoor types with their cut lunches or their fruit. Notwithstanding, there is a new generation of city dwellers who have no affinity for the country. Confirmed urbanites, they pack the quick-lunch places, the tavern bars, and the restaurants. The pioneer people are becoming sophisticated in yet another way.

Even so, cities do not seem to shape people
here in New Zealand. They merely colour
the shape already imposed by the land and the
past. Auckland, as the largest city, imposes on
its inhabitants a special colour—it is no deeper
than that—which makes them, while they
remain inhabitants of that city, recognisably
Aucklanders. They enjoy a life-style not
matched by other towns. Auckland is warm and
bright and lively. So are Aucklanders. They
do things in a way that is their very own.
Auckland houses seldom seem to have that careful tidiness that you see in Christchurch homes,
nor the wealth of heirloom furniture, still
unthinkingly used, that Dunedin homes so

often have. They are places for eating and
sleeping in, albeit comfortable, well furnished,
for the utmost convenience; usually modern at
least in room and furniture arrangement, for
Aucklanders are people who spend a large
proportion of their time out of doors. They are
in love with their harbour, and rightly so,
for it is beautiful and broad and not too
cluttered with shipping. They swim in it and
yacht on it and water-ski over it and fish in it.
They have a greater wealth and variety of
evening amusements than other New Zealand
cities, simply because they support them.
There are more people to do so, for one thing,
and their climate, even in mid-winter, is easier
to go out in.

You can go along Auckland's Tamaki Drive, one of the busiest and most lovely out-of-city-centre, harbourside thoroughfares, and find stalls on the roadside selling fresh fish. In Queen Street, shopkeepers and assistants will come out of their shops to entice window-gazers inside. In fact, in everything, Aucklanders come out to meet you, whether it be to sell to you, or to entertain you or simply to invite you to dinner.

Wellington is almost as cosmopolitan as Auckland, by Aucklanders' admission. If any-thing, it is rather more so, in fact. Being the nation's capital, its streets hear almost every major language on earth being spoken. Turbans and sarongs and saris are often seen. It is noisy, cheerily so.

But the most striking fact which is borne upon the visitor to Auckland and, to a slightly lesser extent, Wellington, is that New Zealand, for all its European population predominance, is indivisibly a part of Polynesia. Maoris one sees in thousands; shop workers, factory workers, soldiers, policemen, sailors, office workers. They emerge at around 5 o'clock from their places of work, which range from garages, bus stations, and factories to law offices, architects' studios, and dental and medical surgeries.

CITY STREET SCENES: ". . . shop workers, factory workers, soldiers, policemen, sailors, office workers . . ."

"... not the only representative of Polynesia ..."

This, incidentally, is a relatively new situation. In the not-too-distant past, Maoris were mostly a rural people, working on the land, in the forests, and on the roads. Since the late 1950s, however, there has been a great migration to the cities, and this has presented the Maori with a whole host of new challenges. To obtain his rightful share of the country's material prosperity, he has had to make a conscious effort to come to terms with the Pakeha concept of individual possession. The old, easy-going communal life of the pa does not put much bread on the table, in European urban society. The Maori has had to make a special effort to improve his formal education, to acquire new skills. It *is* a challenge, for New Zealand is, and has long been, a predominantly European society with a predominantly European culture. The Maori has resisted any trend towards the complete submersion of his culture; and while he is entering more and more into those trades and professions which were once an almost totally European preserve, he is not doing so at the expense of his Maori identity. The Maori lawyer's learning has not been acquired, nor his dignity assumed, at the

expense of his Maori heritage. He is still, nevertheless, a Maori. For this is a bi-cultural society, wherein the two cultures interlock rather more than they abrade each other.

But the Maori is not the only representative of Polynesia in New Zealand society. On Queen Street in Auckland, and Manners and Willis Streets in Wellington, one sees the brown faces and wide, white smiles of Samoans, Cook Islanders, and other Polynesians, who have perhaps, been forced from their homelands by economic pressures as surely as the old-time

Maori was forced from his by expanding population pressures, but finding, as he did not, a settled and friendly land in which to live.

Wellingtonians, like Aucklanders, are in love with their harbour, enormous but not so wide and wandering as Auckland's Waitemata. They live on steep hillsides around it, in curious old Victorian villas, in modern apartment blocks which seem to cling precariously to the steep faces, and in perfectly normal New Zealand bungalows standing on flat shelves. Many of them live in the hills behind the city's harbourside heart, often in little hanging valleys which are filled delightfully with native bush, and native birds. Wellingtonians tend not to be gardeners, as Christchurch people are—and this, though a generalisation, is a safe and sound one, for so much of their land is too vertical for gardening. But they are garden lovers. Yet perhaps the reason is not so much because of their severely sloping sections, as because few Wellingtonians seem to have been Wellingtonians born and bred. In a city which contains the head offices of so many of the country's larger businesses, as well as the seat of Government and a vast army of civil servants, a goodly share of the city's population consists of people who have been transferred to Wellington during the pursuit of their various careers. Most are fond of, even enthusiastic about, Wellington, but it might well be argued that most of them, in a set-aside back corner of their hearts, still regard themselves as being people of Masterton or Marton or Wanganui or Bulls or Hastings, rather than as being true Wellingtonians, and have firm intentions of some day going back to their respective home-towns. Few do, but the dream is there; and for this reason, perhaps they think that they merely tolerate Wellington, live in high-rise apartments or old, sub-divided mansions or gardenless hillside homes which would require an immediate fortune or a lifetime of devoted effort to landscape.

So they wander in their thousands through the beautiful botanical gardens, and maybe dream of the day when they will grow their own roses in Stratford or Manaia.

WELLINGTON HARBOUR: ". . . curious old Victorian villas, modern apartment blocks which . . . cling precariously to the steep faces . . ."

". . . grow their own roses in Stratford or Manaia.

SUBURBAN SUPERMARKET.

Christchurch people are definitely gardeners. In a city, most of which is utterly flat, gardening is not difficult. Aucklanders tend to believe that the Christchurch climate precludes the growing of any but hardy plants. In truth, however, Christchurch's temperatures, except in mid-winter, are seldom far below those of Auckland, and, in high summer, often top the northern heat. There is less humidity, and therefore less of a greenhouse feeling about Christchurch hot days than there is in Auckland. Magnolias are grown in Christchurch. Rhododendrons and azaleas flourish. Grapes grow happily out of doors. and one keen Christchurch gardener has nourished a banana plant—inside. Christchurch, with its quarter-million population, is still, endearingly, a provincial town; or, rather, it is an overgrown country town. Aucklanders live within their own suburbs, well served by shopping centres, and many seldom go into the Queen Street area, unless it is to work in a shop or office there. Christchurch people, whether they work near the centre of town or not, mostly go there at least once a week—usually Friday night, the

DOWNTOWN STORE.

late shopping night. They enjoy good suburban shopping facilities, but still, for one reason or another, "go to town" regularly and often.

Dunedin, smallest of the four main centres, preserves a way of life that is fast disappearing, even in Christchurch. Dunedin people do most of their shopping and other business in the George Street - Octagon - Princes Street centre of their town. Though they, like Wellingtonians, build their houses on steep hillsides, they are more often than not keen and clever gardeners.

DUNEDIN SUBURBAN STREET: ". . . a quality of life . . ."

Dunedin people often seem to be quieter, more thoughtful than the people from farther north. They have clung to old values—not because they have been accidentally left behind in the "progress" scramble, but because it is their deliberate policy—yet another generalisation, but again, a fair one, which speaks of the majority of Dunedin people. They enjoy a quality of life, an absence of disturbing change, which is reflected in their well-preserved old family homes, in their ability to create their own amusements. They have all the amenities, all of the comforts that citizens of other centres enjoy, but they themselves do not change, essentially.

The fact is, they still enjoy an illusion of isolation. You can approach Dunedin from the north by sailing up a long, narrow harbour, along a channel which twists amongst sandbanks; or you can climb over your pick of two high hills, the usual choice being the motorway, which is a long haul up to the top, followed by an exceedingly steep run down into the hill-girt city; or you can fly in, to be landed at an airport which is some considerable distance to the south of the city. In their snug basin between the mainland hills and the high ridges of Otago Peninsula, and in their suburbs amongst the bush-clad steeps, they might well set their own pace, and can afford to ignore the clamour of the new-rich north, they whose great grandparents were living in solid, well-appointed, civilised houses when the northern settlers were still making do with slab huts and flax-thatched whares. There is a quiet in their faces, and assurance in their manner which is refreshing and, somehow, reassuring.

CHAPTER 4

The New Zealand Evening

Naturally enough, it is in the evening that the
New Zealander's growing sophistication is most
evident. Evenings find him spending con-
siderably less time at the family fireside than
was usual even 10 or 15 years ago. He goes
out more, enjoys an ever-widening range of
cultural pursuits and amusements. And here
yet again, the recent pioneer past reveals itself
in the New Zealander's cultural pursuits and
amusements.

His attitude to art, for example, would be
typical. One is given talent, he feels, to enable
one to accomplish some definite aim. Thus, if
a man has an aptitude for wielding pencil and
brush, its obvious employment is in the production of pictures. Pictures, the New Zealander
feels, are a means of bringing into the living
room a life-like representation of a person
or scene or object of which one is fond, but
the original of which cannot for obvious reasons
be carried into the house, or preserved

SHOTOVER RIVER, CENTRAL OTAGO: ". . . appeals to a man's innate sense of beauty."

MATUKITUKI VALLEY, WANAKA DISTRICT, CENTRAL OTA

indefinitely as it is at the time when one finds it most enjoyable. A view of Mount Aspiring, seen across Lake Wanaka, appeals to a man's innate appreciation of beauty. He cannot stand there looking across Lake Wanaka forever, so he looks for a painting of it, to hang in his house (he usually prefers a painting to a photograph, because the painting, if it is good, captures the essential view, with its subtleties of light and distance and perspective, whereas a photograph lays it out in its actuality, like a pictorial catalogue of the scene; he usually could not express this in so many words, but that, by and large, is his feeling about it.)

Therefore, he gives the artist a reason for painting Mount Aspiring, or Aunt Maggie, or a 4½-litre supercharged 1930 Bentley. He wants to be able to look at it, with all the features of it that appeal to him, at any hour of the day or night. The picture must therefore communicate these features in such a way as to speak to his emotions in the same way in which the original does. If it can do that, it is a job—a good, competent piece of craftsmanship; and that he can readily understand. Craftsmanship is admired. It is useful. The craftsman earns his bread.

The abstract, the use of colour and form for the sake of colour and form, leaves the average New Zealander somewhat cold. It is not that he is incapable of understanding it. It is just that both the artist and John Citizen start at a disadvantage; and that is where that pioneer past makes its presence felt. The pioneers had little time for the finer, gentler things of life. A man, to be worth the precious bread he ate, had to be able to get and hold a roof over his family's head, and to produce food, and supply clothing. He had to be facile with an axe, saw, hammer, hoe, spade, rifle, and knife. In the gentler parts of the country, such as Canterbury and the northern parts of Otago, pioneer existence tended to be a little less rigorous (and the settlers often a little more cultured, and sometimes wealthier) than in other areas. They could indulge their artistic appreciation with imported works; and they informed the tastes of their countrymen, not

always well. There was simply little or no contact with artistic development overseas, and no encouragement at all for peculiar people who wanted to mess around with paint. Water colour for the ladies, yes. Oils and sketching for a hobby, perhaps; but—

The flowering of artistic progress in New Zealand probably dates from the late 1940s, and the citizenry at large simply have not caught up with it.

There is a great need for someone who has been part of the movement, and who is sufficiently articulate, not merely in the jargon of painting, sculpture, and art criticism, but in plain, honest English—someone who can resist the temptation to assume an attitude of "oh, they will never understand it, so what is the use." Such a person could do much to bridge the widening gulf between artist and the general public.

"Some subtlety of form or texture, some cunning contrivance of light

One sees New Zealanders in art galleries, staring blankly at an abstract work, or brows furrowed in a fierce glare, rather resentful that it should present itself for admiration or intelligent comment, yet make no attempt, apparently, to communicate. Yet when, as sometimes happens, the artist himself can point out some subtlety of form or texture, some cunning contrivance of light from coloured pigment, and say:
"I struggled for days (or weeks or months) to achieve that effect," most people understand. It really does dawn on them that there is a man who set out to do something incredibly difficult, and with skill, patience, and infinite labour, managed to accomplish it. That, they can appreciate, exactly as they can appreciate the fact that some ancient Greek, working with chisels on steely marble, achieved an airy flow of draperies. When they can appreciate that, they can enjoy paintings for what they are, and not merely for what they represent. They become not factual representations of scenes, people, and things, but little miracles of colour, texture, form, and light. And that could be the beginning of a golden age for New Zealand artists.

"Theatre is slowly emerging . . ."

"A reason for painting

The theatre and literature deserve the same kind of bridge. Literature is, indeed, flourishing. New Zealanders have produced an astonishing volume of good books and plays in the past 20 years. But the average man-in-the-street New Zealander still opines that the only really useful sphere of endeavour for a writer is journalism; and he has been so starved of live theatre for so long, and disappointed time and time again by the amateurism which pervades home-grown theatre, that he prefers to take his entertainment at the cinema. (By amateurism, one means the attitude of mind which says, of a novel one is writing or a play one is producing: "This is pretty good—for me. After all, I am only a part-timer").

Theatre is slowly emerging from this state. There are some quite superb New Zealand actors and actresses who, though acting on a part-time basis, turn in a truly polished performance. There are some—very few—good producer-directors. But there are not so many that the public stands in danger of becoming theatre minded.

There seems to be a sort of intellectualism in our approach to serious theatre—an insistence on educating which is placed before entertaining. Perhaps, until drama becomes more dramatic, and comedy more generally amusing, live theatre will continue to languish.

This opinion seems to be borne out by the fact that a company putting on Victorian melodrama, inviting audience participation in the form of hissing and booing the villian, and responding to heroic "asides to the audience," attracted crowds unfailingly; and most cities and many smaller towns have an operatic society putting on regular musical shows and operettas which enjoy weeks-long seasons with good houses. And that is no mean feat, where populations are small—where even the largest city, Auckland, has a population numbering a bare half-million.

THEATREGOERS: ". . . rather Elizabethan in his approach to theatre."

The fact is, New Zealanders are fun-loving. They do not wish to take their theatre seriously, nor to endure endless agonised moralisings from the stage. They simply wish to be entertained with reasonably smooth, professional productions. The New Zealander is, perhaps, rather Elizabethan in his approach to theatre. He turns up in his workaday suit, as a general rule, and expects to be diverted for perhaps 2 hours, with an interval in the middle when he may go out to the foyer for a smoke and a chat (smoking is prohibited inside New Zealand theatres, thankfully). He may, alternatively, sit in his seat and consume ice cream; and during the show, he refreshes himself unabashedly with sweets. He likes a belly-laugh, and his drama

needs to be highly coloured. He is, generally, a mannerly audience, however. He is not demonstrative, and a standing ovation is something of a rarity. By the same token, he cannot usually bring himself to dismiss a mediocre performance without a polite hand-clap, and he rarely walks out, even from an embarrassingly poor show. He will walk out on an obviously rude or insulting attitude displayed by a performer.

Critics fail to influence him. Big names do. Audiences differ from city to city. The Aucklanders will turn out to a good, colourful, noisy "Taming of the Shrew" type of comedy, preferably by an untested playwright, which has

NEW ZEALAND NATIONAL ORCHESTRA.

never been able to find a producer in Dunedin. It is not the content of the play, or even the type of play, that makes the difference. Dunedin will applaud a painstaking, polished performance. Small towns will fill the local theatre to see a visiting company which may fail to attract an audience in the cities—in which New Zealanders are perhaps no different from any other people.

Generally speaking, the kiwi's small-town pioneer society background still tends to colour his tastes, which is only natural; and it is probably a good thing, because there are signs of a distinct, home-grown culture emerging out of his attempts to find and meet preferences in art, music, literature, the performing arts, and even cuisine.

"Diners . . . have a choice of reasonable to good restaurants . . . and they are becoming more knowledgable about win[e]"

Perhaps an even more encouraging sign is the number of young Maoris who study at the New Zealand Maori Arts and Crafts Institute at Rotorua, and under many independent masters, to revive the ancient crafts of their people; or, rather, to keep them alive, for they have never been allowed to die. Many study the once languishing Maori language at school and in extension study courses at the universities (astonishingly, and as an indication of the inter-locking nature of the two cultures, one-third of the 5,500 secondary school students studying Maori are Europeans!).

Clearly, whatever form the emerging culture takes, it will be strongly influenced by Maoritanga the culture and very meaning of Maori. And in that, it will be a unique thing indeed.

On the subject of cuisine, diners in the cities now have a choice of reasonable to good restaurants, no matter what the food snob some-times says to the contrary; and they are becoming more knowledgable about wines. Thirty years ago wine meant to the average, untravelled New Zealander the fortified sherries he offered his guests as an almost inevitable aperitif, and the fortified port-type wines to which the older generation treated itself at Christmas and on special occasions. Today, he has a small repertoire of wines which he enjoys himself, and serves or recommends to his friends; and there are New Zealand connoisseurs of some standing.

On the subject of wines, New Zealand, from time to time, suffers from the kind of guest who, weaned on Chablis and Bordeaux and Burgundy, Sauterne, Moselle, and Medoc of Europe, damns our wines with faint praise, or is condescendingly condemnatory about them. Wisely, however, New Zealand vintners continue along their chosen paths of develop-ment, not striving for a carbon copy of Chateau-d'Yquem or a Hochheim, but evolving a wine which is top-quality and of a character un-matched anywhere else; a national wine capable of earning an international reputation—as some already have.

The New Zealander—the new, more sophisticated New Zealander—still enjoys his spectator sports with all of his old gusto, but now he has added squash courts and badminton halls to his list of sporting amenities; and at floodlit trotting track and athletic stadium, enjoys in the evenings sports once reserved for Saturday afternoons.

The sporting New Zealander is often accused by his less sport-orientated countrymen of being not so much sports-minded as sports-worshipping. His religion, it is said consists of rugby, racing, and beer. The accusation leaves him profoundly unmoved—and it is something of a cheap jibe, because he knows where his sport ends and his workaday life begins.

"Sporting New Zealander . . ."

"The thing is a game, after all,

For example, though rugby fans stand jam-packed, shoulder to shoulder, crammed on a wind- and rain-swept embankment to watch a rugby match for which they have queued for hours, they do not, customarily, resort to hurling bottles at the referee when the home team is beaten. The thing is a game, after all, and while it may be an important enough slice of life to be prognosticated upon, conjectured over and conversed about almost to the exclusion of all other topics, winning or losing is hardly a matter of life or death. A team—and its supporters—are out for a win but, thankfully, the game is still the thing. If it were not, New Zealand cricketers would never have continued to sally forth to play the West Indies or the M.C.C; and soccer, which is virtually 100 percent post-war in its following, would never have dared to take on a professional overseas team with high records going back the greater part of a century.

BROOD MARES, WAIKATO RACING STUD, NORTH ISLAND: "New Zealand
horses, pasture-fed and hardy . . ."

Racing, of course, is in a slightly different category. In the final analysis, the horse does the work, and New Zealand horses, pasture-fed and hardy, have something of a stamina advantage, often enough, over overseas horses. But the same principle stands. The game is the thing.

The New Zealander, during spring and summer evenings, mows his suburban lawns, usually with a motor mower, these days. He does not tinker with his own car to the extent that he used to. His wife ventures forth on spring evenings to Ikebana flower arranging classes, or to pottery lessons; and her husband goes to squash, because today's sedentary life demands a regular programme of deliberate physical exercise.

On the farms tucked away in the green hills, though, wives and daughters still feed orphaned lambs from bottles; and the orchardist sits up late, attending to his smoke pots, contending with the late frosts that his fathers knew and suffered.

Summer still sees families enjoying an evening riverside or seaside picnic, but the English hamper has largely given way to the American barbecue.

SHEEP COUNTRY, WAIPUKURAU, HAWKE'S BAY: ". . . farms tucked away in the green hills . . .".

LIGHTS ON THE HARBOUR BRIDGE, AUCKLAND.

FIREWORKS ON THE MARINE PARADE, NAPI

Yet, never far from the bright lights and sophistication is the old, untamed New Zealand, where the mysterious night forest still whispers secretly to itself as it did before man ever set foot on these islands, and the flightless kiwi still pursues his nocturnal prowlings and peckings, and nameless streams still rattle past the brooding trees.

Strangely though, people move around in the bush much more today, than ever before. In pioneering times, it was either dangerous with lurking enemies, or it was a man's work place, and thus not appreciated for what it is, a place of marvellous beauty. Today, it is often a playground. People go to it at night, across the midnight-black, glinting waters of Lake Te Anau, to the Alice-in-Wonderland adventure of a trip into a forest cave; or they walk up marked paths in the almost subtropical bush about the

foot of the Fox Glacier, to see displays of glowworms, small, blue constellations in the banks beneath the close-woven trees.

For the children, summer evenings' activities begin, really, with Guy Fawke's night, 5 November, when they stay up late to prance around bonfires on beaches or in country paddocks or stand tip-toe with excitement around suburban back lawns to watch father set off fireworks, in memory of gunpowder, treason, and plot. They can usually tell you, when asked, a more or less accurate version of the great plot; but poor Guido Fawkes, whom they burn in effigy on their fires, arouses no hatred or fear in them. If anything, they rather like him for giving them this night, and would probably admit that he ranks next in their esteem to Father Christmas.

TROUT FISHERMAN, OTAGO: ". . . has the peaceful, willow-flanked lakes and riverbeds to himself at last .

Summer nights are spent out of doors, in holiday time. Pony trekkers sing beside mountain-valley camp fires, and yachtsmen lounge in cockpits off Kawau Island, their craft riding easily at anchor flirting their slim bows at the Mansion House, whose lights are yellow in the languorous night.

But as autumn sets in, fewer people take their pleasures outside. The angler still does, for now the last of the evening picnickers and weekend campers have gone home for the winter, and he has the peaceful, willow-flanked lakes and riverbeds to himself at last, to flick his dry fly out amongst the swarming gnats, dropping it lightly onto the water, to tempt the evening-rising trout.

In New Plymouth, on the North Island's westernmost cape, people gather at Brooklands Bowl for the Festival of the Pines, with its rich offerings of Shakespeare of England, the ballets of Russia, and the music of France, Germany, Poland, and Italy, heard and seen across a mirror of a lakelet and a tamed but still native landscape.

In flat Manawatu stock-car racing enthusiasts flock in crowds to thrill to their favourite spectator sport.

In Napier, on the east coast, it is still warm enough for people to stroll, of an evening, along the Marine Parade, where the giant Norfolk Pines are ablaze with coloured lamps, like huge Christmas trees, or to watch from their hill the last of the season's yachts coming in across the flaming water of the bay, as the sun sets.

SKIERS, CHATEAU TONGARIRO, NORTH ISLAND: ". . . a cosmopolitan air of *apres-
a heady mixture of log fires, colourful Fairisle jerseys, cocktails, beer, and loud pop mus

Footballers of all three persuasions, association, rugby, and league, are working up as a team beneath floodlights, breath pluming on the cold, evening air.

In Mangonui, Northland, a group of Maoris gathers in the waterfront pub to drink beer and play English darts.

Even winter fails to discourage evening outings. Winter, of course, is the season of balls and dine-and-dance evenings—special occasions, to be dressed up for. The theatres attract their crowds, even though "theatre" is still the fad of the few, and cinema reigns supreme.

In Queenstown, that small alpine village, in its hotels and motels, and in luxurious mountain-chalet holiday houses at Kelvin Heights, across the Frankton Arm of Lake Wakatipu, there is a cosmopolitan air of *apres-ski*, a heady mixture of log fires, colourful Fairisle jerseys, cocktails, beer, and loud pop music.

"... enjoying last drinks ..."

On the inter-island ferry, as it slips silently through the misty night, the watch on the bridge, faces reflected like deep-shadowed ghosts in the window glass, stare ahead into the black night. Below, late-retiring passengers sip beer in the saloon, or conclude a meal, or watch television, or take a last turn around the decks, pausing and peering towards the land, and perhaps seeing, far off to the west, a moon-limned ghost of some lofty, snow-crowned alpine ridge.

Between the ship and those peaks, there are people dancing, people enjoying last drinks before the pubs close, people eating, people working, playing, writing, making love, crooning over a restless baby, tending the sick, giving last rites to the dying, driving ambulances, chairing the meetings of a hundred town and county councils; all over the country they are doing these things, from Kaitaia in the far north to tiny Oban on Stewart Island in the distant south. They are reading, singing, playing

MT. NGAURUHOE: "The New Zealand evening . . ."

jangling guitars, bowing mellow violins, arguing a Bill through Parliament, standing guard. Yet already, many are folding newspapers, closing books or writing pads, turning off TV and radios, putting cats out and taking milk bottles to the gate, putting spark guards in front of dying fires, and preparing for bed; because, with all the changes and fashions, one pioneer habit still lingers amongst the majority. New Zealanders are not, even now, a late-night people.

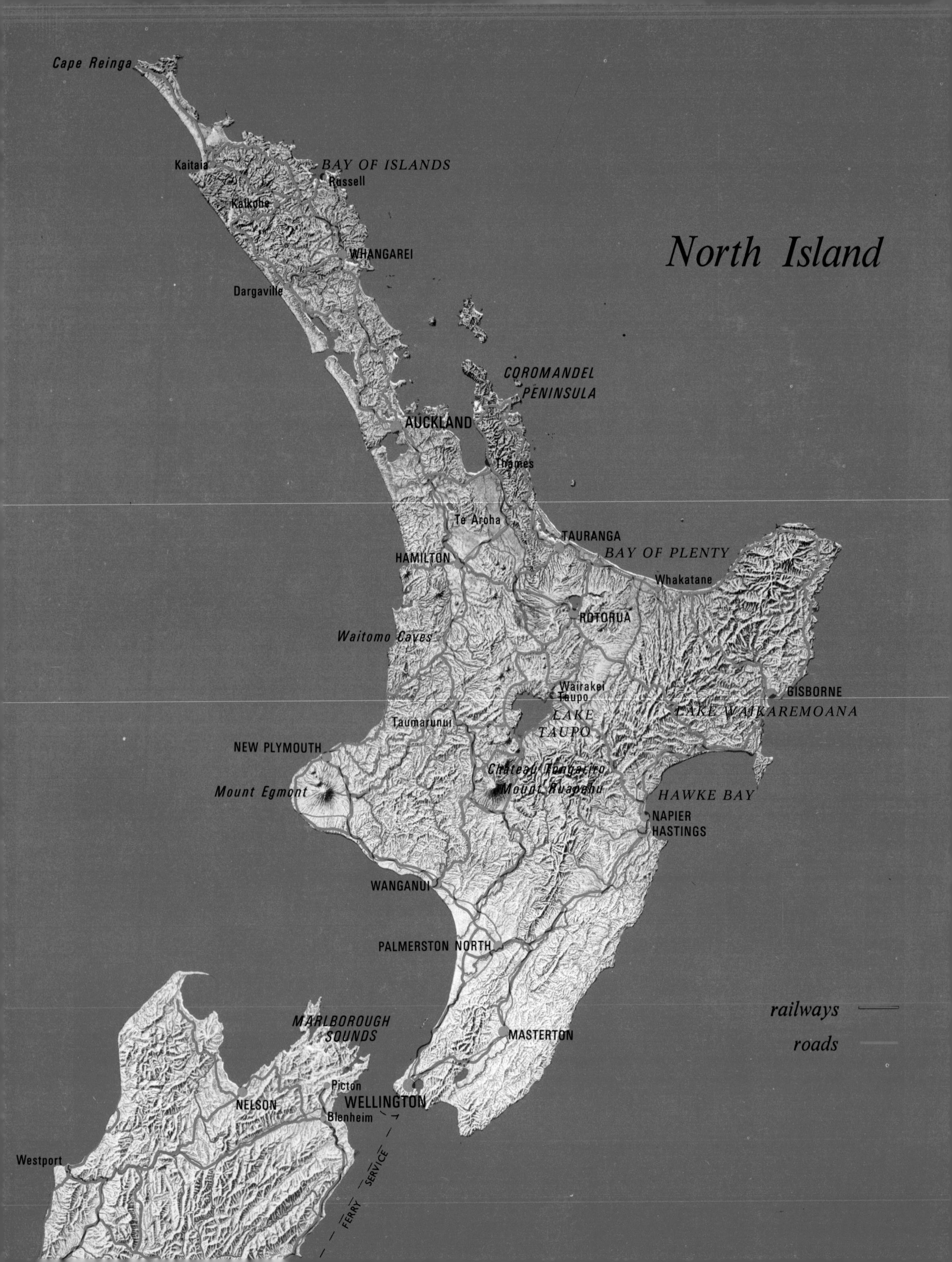

North Island

Cape Reinga

Kaitaia
BAY OF ISLANDS
Kaikohe
Russell

WHANGAREI

Dargaville

*COROMANDEL
PENINSULA*

AUCKLAND

Thames

Te Aroha
TAURANGA
HAMILTON
BAY OF PLENTY
Whakatane

ROTORUA

Waitomo Caves

Wairakei
Taupo
GISBORNE
LAKE WAIKAREMOANA
Taumarunui
*LAKE
TAUPO*

NEW PLYMOUTH

Chateau Tongariro
Mount Ruapehu
HAWKE BAY
Mount Egmont
NAPIER
HASTINGS

WANGANUI

PALMERSTON NORTH

*MARLBOROUGH
SOUNDS*
MASTERTON

railways

roads

Picton
NELSON
WELLINGTON
Blenheim

Westport

FERRY SERVICE

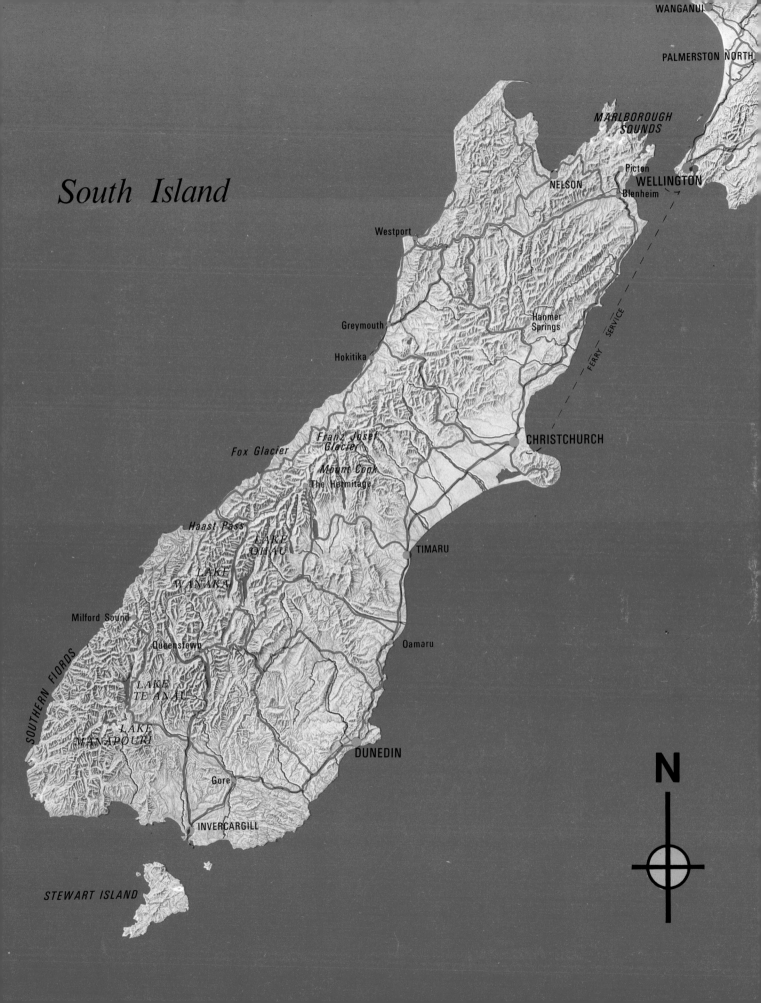

Epilogue

What remains to be said? What, after all, is New Zealand like? It is a beautiful country in a largely beautiful world. Within its three main islands, it packs practically every type of scenery that the world can offer. Much of it is rugged country, unforgiving if you misjudge its strength or its temper; yet it is still a demi-Eden, for its climate is seldom savage, and it harbours no venomous creatures (except the tiny katipo spider, first cousin to the Black Widow—and even he is confined largely to piles of driftwood on lonely beaches). Its only dangerous wild animals are the rangy, razor-back Captain Cooker pigs which roam the crumpled ranges, and the roaring-season stag; and these are seldom aggressive.

Therefore, as you might expect, the people are generally kindly, a little hard to read, not giving themselves readily, yet seldom antipathetic towards strangers. They are strong, not easily swayed, particularly the country people, who seem to be commanded to benevolence by the power of those lofty, watching hills; although to attribute kindliness solely to a country upbringing would give a false impression, and, in any case, the history of European habitation is still short enough for everyone to have some sort of roots in, or some connection with, the country.

Perhaps, then, the whole thing is best summed up by repeating that New Zealanders are what the land has made them. No other influence has been so strong.

A. R. SHEARER, GOVERNMENT PRINTER, WELLINGTON, NEW ZEALAND—1974

24751H—73 D

TOKYO
HONG KONG
MANILA
BANGKOK
SINGAPORE
S O U T H
SYDNEY
MELBOURNE
AUCKLAND
NEW ZEALAND
WELLINGTON
CHRISTCHURCH
DUNEDIN